Black and Smart

The American Campus

Founded by Harold S. Wechsler

The books in the American Campus series explore recent developments and public policy issues in higher education in the United States. Topics of interest include access to college; college affordability; college retention, tenure and academic freedom; campus labor; the expansion and evolution of administrative posts and salaries; the crisis in the humanities and the arts; the corporate university and for-profit colleges; online education; controversy in sport programs; and gender, ethnic, racial, religious, and class dynamics and diversity. Books feature scholarship from a variety of disciplines in the humanities and social sciences.

For a list of all the titles in the series, please see the last page of the book.

Black and Smart

How Black High-Achieving
Women Experience College

ADRIANNE MUSU DAVIS

Rutgers University Press

New Brunswick, Camden, and Newark, New Jersey
London and Oxford

Rutgers University Press is a department of Rutgers, The State University of
New Jersey, one of the leading public research universities in the nation. By
publishing worldwide, it furthers the University's mission of dedication to
excellence in teaching, scholarship, research, and clinical care.

Library of Congress Cataloging-in-Publication Data

Names: Davis, Adrianne Musu, author.

Title: Black and smart : how Black high-achieving women experience
college / Adrianne Musu Davis.

Description: New Brunswick : Rutgers University Press, [2023] | Series:
The American campus | Includes bibliographical references and index.

Identifiers: LCCN 2022037741 | ISBN 9781978832374 (Paperback :
acid-free paper) | ISBN 9781978832381 (Hardback : acid-free paper) |
ISBN 9781978832398 (epub) | ISBN 9781978832411 (pdf)

Subjects: LCSH: African American women—Education (Higher) |
African American college students—Social conditions. | Gifted women—
Interviews. | Discrimination in higher education—United States.

Classification: LCC LB2341 .D34 2023 | DDC 378.1/982996073—dc23/
eng/20230104

LC record available at https://lccn.loc.gov/2022037741

A British Cataloging-in-Publication record for this book is available
from the British Library.

References to internet websites (URLs) were accurate at the time of writing.
Neither the author nor Rutgers University Press is responsible for URLs that
may have expired or changed since the manuscript was prepared.

♾ The paper used in this publication meets the requirements of the
American National Standard for Information Sciences—Permanence of
Paper for Printed Library Materials, ANSI Z39.48-1992.

rutgersuniversitypress.org

For my brilliant Black girls, Raven Phylicia and Ella Jade.
My gratitude for the talented Black women who trusted me
with their stories and illuminated the way for the ones
who will next walk their paths.

Contents

Black and Smart

Students Like Jada

Invisible High-Achieving Black Women

Before Jada came to my office one quiet afternoon, we had never shared more than a smile in the hall or a passing hello in the honors lounge. But on that day, near the end of my first year as an academic advisor, Jada came to the office and requested to meet with me because she needed more than academic advising. She sat in the quilted khaki armchair on the other side of my desk, introduced herself as a junior communications major, then sank down a bit as she recounted what happened in her honors course in a classroom just down the hall from my office.

She and her classmates were seated around the seminar table. Her classmate John made insensitive generalizations about Black students who were not in honors courses; during class discussion he commented that they probably should not be in college anyway. As the only woman of color in a classroom full of academically talented students, Jada felt under fire. Most of her friends at college were not honors students, especially her friends of color. And they had the same right to be at college as everyone else, honors or not. Despite the anger and hurt rising inside her, she spoke up and addressed his comments directly and calmly. She pointed out that John spent most of his time with other honors students who were from his same ethnic background and that he did not know enough about all Black students at the university to make such a statement. Then there was silence. After her retort, none of her classmates spoke up to support her assertions. Nobody said anything at all. The silence felt deafening. And especially frustrating was the silence from the head of the seminar table. Her instructor chose not to intervene or to address either Jada's or John's comments. He moved on with class indifferently.

As she continued sharing, I learned that this was not a one-time occurrence for Jada. Her White peers and professors dismissed her perspectives in other classes as well, even when she cited the text or shared from personal experience, and even in her honors classes. Their disregard for her insights made her feel angry, unsupported, and unheard. Like most of her peers, Jada was admitted into honors because of her high standardized test scores and excellent grades. She was bright and book smart, and she spoke like it. And by the measures that earned them all entry into that class, she was just as intelligent as her peers. She had the same right to learn and contribute as everyone else yet constantly felt pressure to prove that she was smart enough to be there, that she belonged in honors as much as the peers who made her question her place. And she felt I was the only person that would understand her situation. My mission began.

Hearing about Jada's experience compelled me to learn about the challenges Black honors women face and to develop strategies to support their success. Jada's experiences reflected issues that required additional attention in higher education research, including cultural insensitivity in the classroom, a lack of community among students of color, and the challenges of teaching and learning across color lines. As an administrator at the university, I had a duty to support all of my students' success, but as a woman of color, I was personally committed to advocating for the needs of students like Jada and other academically talented undergraduate Black women. My experiences as a Black woman within my race and gender and academic identity groups were important to the way I viewed the world and gave me insight into the racial, gender, and intellectual oppression that students like Jada faced in campus life[1] (Collins, 1991, p. 33).

I put myself in Jada's shoes, wondering how I might have handled a situation like that at her age, how much courage it must have taken to speak up, and the worry of seeking someone for support afterward. I empathized with Jada and her peers and felt a sense of responsibility to help them individually and as a group to overcome the injustices they experienced in campus life. My position as an advisor in the honors program gave me access to the kinds of resources— human and social capital—that would allow me to make a difference in these women's lives. I moved forward with an intervention I hoped would address some of their concerns.

I initiated the Honorables of Color gatherings to provide opportunities for honors students of Black, Asian, Latinx, Native American, Middle Eastern, and multiracial backgrounds to meet each other, share their experiences, and to help them create a sense of community as they supported one another through their college experience. Our bimonthly discussion meetings were relatively informal, starting with icebreakers and then the featured topic for the evening. We chatted about adjusting to college life, garnered advice from upperclassmen on academic success, demystified the networking process, and invited grad students and faculty of color to discuss their career paths and give encouragement. The first meeting had over forty eager participants of all shades of brown, tan, beige, and mahogany skin. It was joyful and we all left smiling, feeling warm and hopeful. But attendance at later sessions dwindled, leaving a modest group of ten Black women as the most consistent participants. In our more intimate group, the discussions consistently came back to the women's concerns about stereotypes associated with their race, gender, and intelligence, and the kinds of situations Jada shared with me when we first connected. They shared their experiences of feeling people's stares during discussions about race in the classroom. They shared feeling unwelcome in the honors lounge because they did not see other students of color there. They were consistently labeled "the Black friend" in their social group without any consideration of their personalities or the other great qualities they could offer. They were accused of "talking White" and so sometimes chose not to talk at all, allowing themselves to be silenced by the threat of others' definition of their identities.

A pivotal moment in my work with the group came from a single question: "Can't I be Black *and* smart?" We were discussing our plans for the next gathering in the honors lounge. I had to sit down. Yes, of course she could! And she didn't need anyone's permission. I wanted to understand what was happening in her life at college that made her sense it was abnormal to be exactly that: Black *and* smart. She could be Black and smart and anything else she dreamed, I thought to myself. This candid question was posed by one of the emerging leaders of the discussion group, and the gravity of the question sparked the specific focus of this book and my future research. The constant battle against racial, gender, and intellectual stereotypes sent these women disturbing messages about their environment. The truth was that these women were capable of portraying intelligence, Blackness, and their gender simultaneously, but their lived reality inside and outside the classroom challenged their ability to confidently embody their overlapping identities.

The experiences of women like Jada inside and outside the classroom revealed the way systems of power in society operated in college life through individual and institutional practices for high-achieving Black women. In consideration of the multifaceted identities of these students and their position at the intersection of overlapping systems of power in society, I understood the importance of not allowing their individual concerns to mask how structural issues in society functioned in campus life inside and outside the classroom. By listening to the stories of high-achieving Black women and using my privilege as a researcher and administrator, I could amplify their voices. I needed to share these uncovered parts of their reality on our campus.

Talented Black Women Matter

The experiences of high-achieving Black women undergraduates were insufficiently studied in higher education (Fries-Britt & Griffin, 2007; Strayhorn, 2009; Sanon-Jules, 2010; Davis, 2018). As Black women, the intersection of racial and gender identities played a role in how they attribute meaning to their experiences as college students and more broadly in the world in a way that differed from their peers (Porter et al., 2020; Njoku & Patton, 2017; Collins, 1991; Banks, 2009; Winkle-Wagner, 2009; West, Donovan, & Roemer, 2009). There were volumes of broad research in the field on how college affected students and the phases of their psychosocial and identity development, and what influenced their success or attrition (Pascarella & Terenzini, 2005; Evans, Forney, & Guido-DiBrito, 1998; Tinto, 1975, 2000), yet high-achieving Black undergraduate women were not the focus of any influential study (Sanon-Jules, 2010; Davis, 2018). Black women were also underrepresented at predominantly White institutions (PWIs), especially among high-achievers (Coleman & Kotinek, 2010). From my experience as an honors administrator, when talented students did get attention, several general assumptions played a role in how faculty and staff approached them as a group. High-achieving Black women's experiences were assumed to be the same as students with similar intellectual and ethnic identities; it was also assumed that their academic talent precluded them from needing resources to be successful. Both assumptions oversimplify the complex issues that resulted from these students' overlapping identities.

Racial identity mattered in the context of Black women's experiences. Some of the problems they faced echo the negative experiences of their non-honors Black peers at PWIs, who also reported experiencing racist microaggressions (Kanter et al., 2017; Swim et al., 2003) and stereotype threat inside and outside the classroom (Lewis et al., 2012; Fries-Britt & Turner, 2001; Spencer et al., 2001; Steele, 2010). The issues facing Black and high-achieving students are unique. The diversity within the group—in social interactions and academic ability, particularly—made it important to examine those differences because not all Black students experience college in the same way (Commodore, Baker, & Arroyo, 2018; Zamani-Gallaher & Polite, 2013; Strayhorn, 2009; Griffin, 2006; Stewart, 2009). Not all Black students were the same nor was every campus; although, as the research above illustrated, there were often consistencies in the hostility of the PWI campus environment.

In practice, all high-achievers—regardless of race, class, or gender—were assumed to face the same issues (or none at all). Despite the intellectual abilities they had in common, high-achievers were not a homogenous population. The ethnic differences within the population meant that academically talented Black students encounter an assortment of challenges at PWIs that differ from their White peers (Strayhorn, 2009; Sanon-Jules, 2010). High-achieving Black students often felt racially isolated on campus and alienated from their majority and other minority peers. Inside and outside the classroom, they experienced subtle and overt forms of racism from peers and instructors. They felt the constant pressure to prove themselves academically (Fries-Britt & Griffin, 2007; Strayhorn, 2009). All of these issues were consistent with Jada and the Honorables of Color concerns. Due to the limited research on this population, there were additional unique issues that had yet to be examined empirically.

Second, while it was clear that at-risk students need resources to succeed, the opposite was often assumed about talented students (Freeman, 1999; Fries-Britt & Griffin, 2007). There were plenty of studies on the best practices of support programs that help underprepared students develop the tools for success at college, even for minority students (Cuyjet, 2006; Gaither, 2005). The federal funding and development of TRIO, Upward Bound, and Educational Opportunity Programs were just a few examples of how institutions across the country supported the needs of underprepared students. They provided specialized academic advising, cultural and social enrichment opportunities, and supplemental instruction to promote academic achievement. From developmental coursework to tutoring services, mentoring programs to comprehensive resource centers, universities actively addressed the needs of their underprepared and high-risk student populations. In contrast, little research advocated for resources to support the needs of students at the other end of the spectrum (Sanon-Jules, 2010). As an honors advisor, I knew academically talented students needed attention too.

The fact that high-achievers were admitted with excellent credentials did not mean they had fewer obstacles to collegiate academic success than their peers (Fries-Britt, 2002; Fries-Britt & Griffin, 2007; Freeman, 1999). Similar to the average college student, high-achieving students also needed support that met their needs. For example, strong academic performance in high school could create the feeling of pressure to perform at high levels in college (Freeman, 1999). And high-achieving students may expect to do well on their own, replicating their high school study habits and learning behaviors that worked at that level. But good high school grades and high SAT scores were not fully indicative of a student's ability to adjust to the expectations of more rigorous academics or campus life outside the classroom. The transition to college may pose unique challenges for this group, some of which could make them at-risk in their own right.

Many honors students maintained high GPAs once they get to college, which is often a requirement to stay in honors. However, the additional challenges facing the Black women were cause for concern: isolation, alienation, and negative interactions with faculty and peers were commonly associated with the experiences of students that leave college (Tinto, 1975; Strayhorn, 2009). Despite their academic talent, the literature suggested that these challenges could put students at risk if their sense of belonging and integration into the campus community did not improve (Strayhorn, 2009). In the interest of the students' future educational outcomes and retention efforts of the university, intentional interventions should be created to address high-achieving Black women's needs. Battling against racial and intellectual stereotypes, these young women were getting the disturbing message from their campuses, and society at large, that it was not okay or possible to be both Black and smart. Something had to be fixed.

Gender also mattered in the context of these students' experiences. Several theorists argued that Black women's positionality made their experiences different than their male peers (West, Donovan, & Roemer, 2009, p. 333). Scholars consistently noted that Black women led their male peers in several areas of higher education (Commodore, Baker, & Arroyo, 2018; Bonner, 2001; Strayhorn & Johnson, 2014). Studies on Black men echoed this perception, noting there were "discernable differences in perceptions and behaviors" (Cuyjet, 2006, p. 21). In this same study on the academic behaviors of African American students, Cuyjet found that Black men demonstrated less frequent note-taking in class, were more likely to use athletic facilities on campus, and were more concentrated in the population of student-athletes than their women counterparts (Cuyjet, 2006, p. 21). Because they fared better than their peers, it was assumed Black women did not need support (Patton & Croom, 2017).

Black women faced several challenges at college. Social homogeneity, isolation, lack of good mentoring relationships, mental health stress, and affording college were among the conditions highlighted in a recent guide to student success for Black women (Commodore, Baker, & Arroyo, 2018). In her study of African American undergraduate women, Winkle-Wagner (2009) found that experiencing culture shock and isolation on campus was common among her participants. There was the "dichotomous pressure to either speak on behalf of their ethnic group or remain silent in the classroom, which forced them to either be in the 'spotlight' or 'be invisible.'" They were stuck in a "dichotomy of racial performance—needing to modify their behavior to neither be 'too White' nor 'too ghetto' (i.e., 'too Black') among their peers" (p. 23). Another study focused on the networks and resources that played a role in student success for Black women in college (Banks, 2009). Informed by a Black feminist lens, Banks focused on cultural capital, oppression at college, support sources, and offers strategies for enhancing care for Black women in college settings. While these issues described Black women broadly, and my research determined that some of the challenges Winkle-Wagner, Banks, and others found applied to the high-achieving population, the lack of research on high-achieving Black women kept the specific differences from their peers of similar race or gender unclear.

Learning more about these students could promote a needed adjustment in the way universities approach supporting this and other minority populations. General resources for Black or students of color broadly were important but may not address Black women's intersecting identities (Everett & Croom, 2017; Patton & Croom, 2017; Porter, 2017; Porter et al., 2020). Much of the college student retention research placed the responsibility for students' integration into campus life and culture in the student's hands. For example, a number of retention scholars posited that students that did not integrate themselves into the campus community would not be successful (Winkle-Wagner, 2009). However, other members of the campus community—including peers and faculty—played a role in creating an environment that welcomed or resisted their identities and customs into campus life. For high-achieving Black college students, acclimation could prove particularly challenging at PWIs. In order to be more inclusive, student cultural background needs to be considered in efforts for retention and academic and social integration. Colleges need to continually learn more about diverse populations to more readily support new groups of students on campus in ways that may differ from the way existing traditional methods allow. For the high-achieving students among them, honors communities and classes could be the place where students feel most welcome or excluded.

To help high-achieving Black women achieve at their highest potential, these misperceptions about their academic abilities and the obstacles that they faced on campus had to be addressed. Black women's unique journeys at college needed more attention (Winkle-Wagner et al., 2019; Banks, 2009; Commodore, Baker, & Arroyo, 2018), and I make the case particularly for students demonstrating academic talent. As a matter of social justice, it was imperative to find ways to provide these students the same opportunities for success as other collegians. At the time of the study, existing research did not provide an understanding of high-achieving Black undergraduate women's experiences in a manner that led to the development of tailored support initiatives. Addressing these students' satisfaction and retention would enable universities to cultivate a capable group of Black professionals to take the lead in society (Fries-Britt, 2002). My research contributes to the knowledge about Black talented undergraduate women to help institutions develop solutions and foster success for them.

There remained limited research that focused specifically on academically talented undergraduate Black women, particularly on their interactions with peers and various others inside and outside the classroom. This lack of knowledge in the higher education community made it challenging for me as an administrator to find ways to support their needs aside from encouraging them to connect with one another and spend more time together socially. Although by nature of their group membership they may have some similarities with their peers, these students' complex intersecting identities made it illogical for me to indiscriminately apply the strategies that may work for Black undergraduates or college women or high-achievers exclusively. Several authors made similar claims about interventions created for Black men, iterating the necessity for campus administrators to learn more about these kinds of students so that appropriate strategies were applied to promote their academic, personal, and social success and to enable other educational professionals to do the same with their own students (Wood & Palmer, 2015; Palmer, Wood, & Arroyo, 2015; Cuyjet, 2006). My research contributes to the knowledge about Black women by illuminating some of the experiences of high-achieving undergraduates absent from consideration in university practice and policy.

Positionality

As a university administrator, I had a duty to support all of my students' success. As an educator of color, I was personally committed to advocating for the needs of students whose voices were often unheard and whose perspectives were unconsidered in campus life. My approach to working with students was shaped by my own positionality.

As a Black woman, my membership in a variety of social groups—race, gender, and class, among others—and their historical significance in American society shape the way I interpret the world. This standpoint and sense of duty carried over into my research. I was once an undergraduate navigating a PWI: some of the experiences that the women share in the pilot research and that are discussed in the literature and in this book resonate with my own. As the conceptual origins of the intersectional framework suggest, my standpoint (and that of the women in this book) as a "Black woman intellectual" may not be accessible to outsiders (Collins, 1991, p. 33). My own personal experiences and perspective brought an acute sensitivity to the experiences of this population that aided my understanding of the nuanced meanings as I collected and analyzed data from student interviews. I could be viewed as an insider by my participants. At the same time, the interviews helped me recognize several social and identity differences I had from the subjects, which were signs of my outsider status.

Helping talented Black women's voices be heard was an act of liberation and quintessential to my research. By centering authentic voices that the academy historically ignored, I hoped to foster conditions in which smart Black women at PWIs can be themselves more fully. My physical appearance may have helped with gaining students' trust as they shared their experiences. My rapport with participants was such that there was an unspoken knowing, that unlike a researcher with a different racial or gender identity, they did not need to be the reluctant educator of all things Black culture with me. I understood from my own experiences that there was more than one way to be Black or woman or any of the other identities we discussed, even when some of the social interactions they told me about suggested the contrary. By undertaking this research, I accepted responsibility for aiding high-achieving Black undergraduate women as a group in their self-definition; however, as with any qualitative study, the researcher as the data collection instrument has to be aware of her biases. As I conducted this research, I bracketed my own perspectives and expectations in an effort to provide a truthful representation of the voices of the academically talented Black women who shared their experiences with me.

The chapters that follow highlight the students' experiences and shed light on the triumphs and challenges of college life for this group of high-achieving Black women undergraduates. Chapter 2 considers identity politics and the intersectional identities and systems of power that influence the students' experiences. Chapter 3 addresses life inside the classroom, including participant interactions with peers and faculty within formal academic settings. Chapter 4 discusses campus life and student interactions outside the classroom with peers and others. Chapter 5 addresses how participants attribute meaning to their identities and their salience across academic and social contexts. Chapter 6 offers implications from the study findings and provides recommendations to enhance university life for high-achieving Black women.

Outline of the Research Project

The purpose of this qualitative study was to understand how academically talented Black undergraduate women attribute meaning to their college experience. Two research questions guided this study: (1) What were the experiences of Black high-achieving college women inside and outside of the classroom at a predominantly White university? and (2) Which aspects of their identity were most salient to the meaning high-achieving Black women made around their experiences in college? After receiving Institutional Review Board approval from my own and the site institutions, data collection took place across two consecutive semesters.

Participants were solicited via email by staff in the honors colleges to current students in their communities at Atlantic University and Polytech University. Respondents shared their background information via a private Google Form. The electronic form collected each student's self-reported personal academic achievement, educational aspirations, socioeconomic status, and self-defined racial or ethnic identity. Students participated in two semistructured interviews on or nearby their campus. Data were analyzed after the first and second interviews to identify codes, create code families, and recognize themes across the students' experiences at college.

As a researcher I recognized that the customary indicators have limitations, particularly applied to students of color but to identify students to participate in the study and to meet the standard practices of research in honors education, I chose honors college membership as the key identifier for high achievement (Borland, 2004; Griffin, 2006; Fries-Britt & Griffin, 2007). There were no more comprehensive or consistent measures available for use at the time. I selected Black women with membership in the honors college because I anticipated they would exhibit a variety of the criteria from the literature to describe their academic talent, including strong secondary school and college GPA and a number of other academic and extracurricular qualifications. My role as an honors administrator also enhanced my access to honors students at other institutions. The appendix includes a full description of the study.

Participant Profiles

JACQUELINE

Twenty-one years old, a senior, and an aspiring graphic designer, Jacqueline had tawny brown skin and very short, thick, curly, natural black hair. She wore artsy, oversized, rectangular, clear-rimmed glasses. Her racer-back bra straps showed above the neckline of her cozy wool-like sweater. She wore mismatched silver and pearl button earrings, a modest silver chain necklace, and grey fitted khaki pants. She described herself as an open-minded, liberal, feminist, young woman college student. She also identified as smart, high-achieving, and gifted.

She was the oldest of two daughters and came from a close-knit African American family. Both her mother and father had completed college, and her younger sister planned to graduate high school early so that she could start college sooner. Her middle-class family lived out of state in the suburbs, not far from a major city. In high school, she spent time with a multicultural group of friends. Her school was mostly White and in a fairly wealthy neighborhood, and she attended as part of a magnet program for her academic interests. She was involved with a women's empowerment group and preprofessional associations at college.

AISHA

Eighteen years old, a freshman, and an aspiring pediatrician, Aisha wore no makeup, had deep brown skin, and wore her curly natural hair pulled up with an afro puff at the top of her head with a stretchy cotton headband. She wore a black hooded jacket with metal snaps and cords that she sometimes pulled at while thinking. She was dressed casually and sat upright, wearing a purple V-neck shirt, infinity scarf, dark blue skinny jeans, and black and silver Toms shoes. She wore button earrings, a metal bracelet with inspirational words on it, and no nail polish. She described herself as an introverted, African American and West African, Christian college student. She also identified as a smart, high-achieving woman.

She grew up as part of a middle-class West African and American family in a small town not far from campus, although she moved around a lot as a child. She was very close with her younger siblings. Her parents were separated and both had graduate degrees; they worked in health care and social work. Aisha was a member of a religious student organization.

SHANTEL

Eighteen years old and a freshman majoring in sociology and humanities, Shantel had light brown skin and wore a buzz cut with a slouchy black skull cap and gold ball stud earrings.

She was dressed almost completely in black, with a fuzzy fleece long-sleeved cotton shirt, velour pants, and patent leather Doc Martens combat boots. She placed her scarf on the table during the interview, focusing her eyes on her fingers playing with the fringe as she spoke without much eye contact. She described herself as an employed Black woman college student who was smart and high-achieving.

Shantel grew up in the same city as the university and enjoyed living at home as a commuter student. She was very independent and had a boyfriend and a very small friend group from high school. She worked about twenty hours a week in food service near campus, which kept her from getting involved at the university. She was a first-generation college student from a middle-class family. Her parents worked in pharmaceuticals and graphic design.

MIRANDA

Twenty years old, a junior, and an aspiring lawyer, Miranda was petite with deep brown skin; straight, relaxed hair past her shoulders; and dark rectangular-framed glasses. She had plain long nails, wore a black and white knit sweater, black leggings, a rose gold watch, and knot-shaped stud earrings. She described herself as a liberal, feminist, young Black woman college student. She also identified as smart, academically talented, straight, and cisgender.

Miranda grew up out of state and abroad as a young child. She lived in a rural small town a few hours from campus during middle and high school. She was the youngest daughter of an upper-class family of West African immigrants. Her parents were divorced, both with graduate degrees, and worked in business and the nonprofit sector. At college, Miranda had a diverse group of friends and was very involved in student life. She was a sorority woman and participated with several preprofessional groups.

SERENA

Nineteen years old, a sophomore, and an aspiring computer scientist, Serena was short with long, dark, straight hair and deep brown skin and manicured eyebrows. She had chipped black nail polish on her fingers and was dressed casually, wearing a black and white striped sweater hoodie, graphic t-shirt, athletic tights, and sneakers. She identified as a Black or West African American woman and an academically talented and gifted, bisexual college student. She also identified as Christian and politically liberal.

Serena was a first-generation American and grew up out of state in an upper-class two-parent household as the oldest of four siblings. Her parents immigrated from West Africa and worked in health care and finance. They both went to college, and her father had a master's degree. Serena also aspired to attend graduate school and to potentially work in health care but was unsure what she might study. She lived on campus and was involved with health care philanthropic, women engineer, and Christian organizations in campus life.

MIA

Nineteen years old, a freshman, and an aspiring health care worker, Mia was petite and sat upright in a feminine, grey, knee-length dress, paisley cream-colored leg warmers, an oversized cream sweater, and black flats. She had light brown skin and her dark brown Senegalese twists dangled just past her shoulders. She described herself as a queer, artsy, Black or Caribbean American woman college student. She also identified as high-achieving and academically talented.

She grew up out of state and her parents were divorced. They immigrated from the Caribbean and neither parent completed college, working in health care and hourly blue-collar jobs. Mia was a first-generation American and college student, hoping to attend graduate school and maybe become a therapist. In high school she was one of two Black girls in her small-town high school magnet program. Mia was involved with service groups on campus.

SHANNON

Twenty-three years old, a fifth-year senior, and an aspiring cyber consultant, Shannon was petite and feminine, sat up straight with very confident posture, and wore a pink knit wrap cardigan with a pink t-shirt and black leggings. She had light brown skin and wore heavy foundation, crisp eyeliner, and nude lipstick. Her tightly curled hair was pinned back from her face, showing her large, white button earrings. She described herself as a Black and Caribbean American woman college student who was athletic, outgoing, and a caring friend. She also identified as smart and high-achieving.

She grew up in a small town out of state in a middle-class family. Her parents were divorced immigrants from the Caribbean. Both attended college, but only one obtained a degree. Shannon was a leader in her sorority and was part of a Caribbean student association and women in STEM groups. She also worked on- and off-campus jobs, went abroad, and had several paid internships during her college years. She had a serious boyfriend and already had a job and relocation plans lined up for after graduation.

MICHELLE

Nineteen years old, a sophomore, and an aspiring speech pathologist, Michelle was petite with tawny brown skin, a round face, and dark brown eyes and wore aviator-shaped glasses near the bottom of her nose. She wore an oversized varsity-style jacket and kept her hands inside the sleeves, a scoop-neck striped t-shirt, jeans, and sneakers. She described herself as a Black woman college student who was straight (but exploring that part of her identity), a Democrat, daughter, and sister. She also identified as high-achieving and academically talented.

Michelle grew up out of state in a small community where she was very socially aware that her family was lower income. Neither parent finished college, and they worked in childcare and in a trade profession. She lived on campus in honors housing. She was involved in several student groups, including philanthropic, Black student, and professional associations, and worked during school breaks.

GRACE

Eighteen years old, a freshman, and an aspiring entrepreneur, Grace had very light brown skin, dark brown eyes, and sandy brown, very curly hair she wore in a ponytail. She had manicured nails, wore a flowery, scoop-neck, short-sleeved sweater with skinny jeans and flats. She identified as a high-achieving Black or mixed race woman college student. She also described herself as optimistic and loving and indicated she ignored most of her other identifiers.

Grace grew up out of state in a small town in an upper-class family. Her parents were Black and White, she had a younger sister, and both parents had completed college—one with a master's degree. She played several musical instruments and was involved with a singing group at college.

AMBER

Nineteen years old, a sophomore, and an aspiring government intelligence officer, Amber had a glamorous weave of shoulder-length wavy hair and wore modest gold button earrings and black eyeliner with no foundation. She had a thin, athletic build and was dressed casually and feminine with a jean jacket, flowery pink printed scarf, black leggings, and lace-up boots. Her backpack had her athletic team logo. Amber spoke confidently and she identified as a smart, high-achieving, Black/West African college student woman. She also identified as liberal and an athlete.

She grew up out of state in an upper-class household, where she lived with her mom. Her parents were divorced, and one had immigrated from West Africa. Both parents had master's degrees and worked for the government. Amber was a Division I student-athlete and was a member of Caribbean student associations.

ANISSA

Eighteen years old, a freshman, and an aspiring pediatrician, Anissa was dressed in a feminine, white, cropped turtleneck sweater and navy pencil skirt with an African printed fabric bangle. She had a dark brown natural-looking weave with a shoulder length twist out and a part to the side. She was soft-spoken but got very excited when discussing her plans for medical school and becoming a doctor. She identified as a high-achieving West African undergraduate woman. She also described herself as Black, Christian, a voracious reader, and family oriented.

She grew up out of state in a small town in an upper-class family. Anissa's parents immigrated from West Africa and both had college degrees, one with a master's. They worked in health care and the tech industry. She was the middle child in her family and was very proud of her older siblings' professional accomplishments. She enjoyed living in honors housing and was involved with several African-oriented, professional student organizations and attended a local church.

NICOLE

Twenty years old, a junior, and an aspiring financial analyst, Nicole had a shoulder-length, natural-looking weave with straight hair, tortoiseshell oval-framed glasses, gold dot earrings, and a modest chain necklace with a pearl. She wore jeans, a long-sleeved white dress shirt, hair ties, and a gold watch on her wrist. Nicole identified as a spiritual, smart, and high-achieving African American/West African undergraduate woman. She also described herself as a liberal, a Democrat, and a Christian.

Nicole grew up out of state in the suburbs with one of her parents as the only child in a middle-class household. Both of her parents had bachelor's degrees. Nicole anticipated graduate school after getting some experience in her field. She enjoyed living off campus that year and being very independent. She was very involved: she worked on campus, did some community service, and had leadership in several professional associations.

ZOE

Nineteen years old, a sophomore, and an aspiring author, Zoe wore a chambray button-down shirt with white polka dots, black leggings, and tall, brown boots. Her natural curly hair was cut in an androgynous short fade, and she wore princess-cut diamond earrings, no makeup, a gold chain with a small charm, and peeling iridescent nail polish. She identified as a smart, high-achieving, Black, African American or Caribbean-American woman college student. She also described herself as a feminist, an artist, a millennial, and her astrological sign and as open minded.

She grew up across town from the university with her mom in an upper middle-class household. Her father was from the Caribbean and lived abroad. Her mother was working on her master's degree and worked in health care. Zoe lived in a house with friends off campus during college. She was involved with a few student groups, including a philanthropy organization.

KESHIA

Nineteen years old, a sophomore, and an aspiring health care professional, Keshia was dressed plainly and casually with a charcoal-colored fleece, jeans, and tall riding boots. She had her relaxed hair in a headband and a low, short ponytail. She pushed the hair behind her ears when she was thinking and pushed her sleeves up often while talking. She wore no makeup or nail polish or earrings. Keshia identified as a smart, high-achieving, African American or Black undergraduate woman. She was also a Democrat and a Lutheran and middle class and straight but felt those identifiers were unimportant. Keshia described herself as a social butterfly, quirky, energetic, and comforting to others.

Keshia was from a rural small town a few hours from campus. She grew up in a lower-class military household with an older sibling. One parent had an associate's degree and the other a GED, and only one was employed. She was involved with her sorority and a professional association and had plans to get more involved with service initiatives.

CRYSTAL

Nineteen years old, a sophomore, and undecided of her career plans, Crystal had her relaxed hair in a short bob and wore no earrings, makeup, or nail polish. She had on a white graphic crop top with a suede-like button-down shirt, and black leggings. She identified as a smart, Black woman undergraduate who felt lost.

She grew up out of state as the middle child of three siblings in an upper-class blended family household. Her parents worked in the communications industry, one with a master's degree and the other some college coursework. Crystal was majoring in computer science but had changed her major six times and was unsure she could graduate in two years if she made many more changes or pursued a minor. She spent most of her time with her boyfriend and did not enjoy living on campus with her messy roommates. She had no other friends but participated in a professional association and attempted to get to know people.

LAURYN

Eighteen years old, a freshman, and aspiring epidemiologist, Lauryn had her dark brown, long, curly hair piled atop her head in a messy bun, and wore silver diamond stud earrings, a nose ring, tortoise shell glasses, and a simple gold chain. She was dressed casually in a blue plaid top, blue tank top, track jacket, sweatpants, and black boots. She sat comfortably, leaned over on the arm of her chair with her legs crossed at the knee. She identified as a high-achieving, upper middle-class, queer, Christian, Black undergraduate woman. She also identified as African American and Creole.

She grew up in the city out of state but moved a few times as a child. Both parents completed college and one had a graduate degree; they worked in education and information technology. They were Creole and Black or African American. At college, Lauryn lived on campus in honors housing. She spent her time working, volunteering, and supporting a women's advocacy group.

~ 2 ~

Beyond Black and Smart

The women at the center of this research project had membership in a number of social groups. As women, high-achievers, and Black students, each of their various social identities played a role in how they made meaning around their experiences in campus life and through which they were subordinated in society within existing systems of power. Each individual facet was important on its own, but as the literature showed, in the lived experiences of Black women, the overlap and mutual influence of these identities and social inequalities was too complex to consider their influences in isolation (Collins, 2015; Winkle-Wagner, 2009; Collins, 1991).

A number of conditions contributed to high-achieving Black undergraduate women's marginalization in college. Campus life mirrored the patterns of racial organization in greater society through its "racial marginalization, racial segregation of social and academic networks" and underrepresentation inside and outside the classroom by faculty and university staff (Steele, 2010, p. 26). These factors remained prominent in the experiences of high-achieving Black women attending PWIs.

As ethnic minorities on campus, Black undergraduates had different experiences than their White peers. Particularly on predominantly White college campuses, the threat of racist behavior toward Black students loomed in the classroom, in interactions with peers, and in campus life. Encountering racism was a part of everyday life for some students (Swim et al., 2003; Sellers & Shelton, 2003; Zamudio & Rios, 2006). Suspicious staring, culturally insensitive comments, and lack of consideration of their opinions were just a few of the racist behaviors Black undergraduates endured from their White peers (Swim et al., 2003; Fries-Britt & Turner, 2001; Sellers & Shelton, 2003). These unwelcoming experiences and the lack of a community of Black peers, faculty, and staff for support made college life isolating and unwelcoming (Fries-Britt & Turner, 2001; Solórzano, Ceja, & Yosso, 2000; Commodore, Baker, & Arroyo, 2018).

The literature refers to some of the offenses above as racist microaggressions, the "subtle and covert ways (i.e. private conversations) that racism manifests itself"; they were the spoken or unspoken judgments others made about Black students' abilities or identities (Solórzano et al., 2000, p. 60; Sellers & Shelton, 2003). Everyday racism was also a common term in the literature and was described as "mundane hassles that could be forgotten by the day's end as well as overt, severe actions" with lasting influence; they were "routine encounters with another's prejudice . . . and discriminatory behavior that pervade people's daily social interactions" (Swim et al., 2003, p. 40).

On an interpersonal level, the cumulative effect of racist interactions made engaging with majority peers tenuous inside and outside the classroom (Swim et al., 2003; Solór-zano, Ceja, & Yosso, 2000; Winkle-Wagner, 2009). The lack of accurate and meaningful incorporation of Black perspectives in the curriculum was not just a source of discouragement for students but a persistent problem in higher education writ large. Racist and discriminatory interactions left students feeling uncomfortable, angry, exhausted, threatened, and continually bothered well after the initial incident (Swim et al., 2003; Solórzano, Ceja, & Yosso, 2000). One study of African American undergraduates' experiences with everyday racism found that over 50 percent of students in the study reached out to friends and family for support after experiencing prejudicial situations. They also found that many Black women responded directly to perpetrators and tended to connect with friends about their situations more often than Black men (Swim et al., 2003). Encounters with racism were common among the academically talented Black women I studied, and my research illuminated how the students navigated their academic and social spaces in the midst of those challenges.

Stereotypes were another issue Black undergraduates faced, as the assumptions others made about Black students in campus life were reflective of the way society viewed those individuals outside its bounds. Stereotypes were not solely a Black issue: any person can feel a threat to their identity based on the social groups to which they belong (Steele & Aronson, 1995). However, Steele argued that women in particular were susceptible, and scholars studying Black women would argue this applies to this group of students in particular. Stereotypes could affect how students developed interpersonally and psychosocially and impact their intellectual performance individually and as a group (Steele, 2010; Jerald et al., 2017). Depictions of Black people in the media as violent or unintelligent, and the especially unfavorable and limited representation of Black women, belied the reality of

Black undergraduates' lives, yet those were the impressions of Black people that they were constantly on guard against (Donahoo, 2017; Porter, 2017). Their concern about potentially embodying the negative stereotypes about their abilities was enough to disrupt their authentic performance of self (Steele, 2010).

The salience of various aspects of students' identities made them susceptible to stereotypes associated with those particular group memberships. Stereotype threat was an identity contingency that constrained people to behave according to the expectations others have for them to reinforce society's perceptions of their membership within a particular identity group. Steele described the power of stereotypes as "floating in the air like a cloud," which "shap[e] our lives and society" (Steele, 2010, p. 7). As Steele argued, this threat could be experienced by anyone with any identity—male, female, Black, young, and so on—but that if these threats were acknowledged, then groups or individuals could take action to change societal expectations and the ways these issues affect individuals.

For high-achieving Black women, their position at the intersection of multiple social groups intensified the potential threat to their identity. For students for whom their intellectual identity was most salient, assumptions people made about their high-achievement ability could adversely affect their performance in private and in public settings (Inzlicht & Ben-Zeev, 2003; Sellers & Shelton, 2003). Research suggested that minority status could be challenging for a member of any group in an environment but particularly for women because of the existence of stereotypes about their abilities (Steele, 2010; Inzlicht & Ben-Zeev, 2003). Students in my study, however, occupied more than one place within the system of power and were multiply influenced by the structural and interpersonal challenges associated with that and other aspects of their identities. In the case of Black high-achieving undergraduate women, others' expectations for their behaviors were reflections of the assumptions society made about numerous aspects of their identities—their Blackness, their gender, and their intellectual ability—in a way that other students did not have to endure. The threat loomed over their interactions with others due to how strongly they felt connected to that identity.

There was heterogeneity in the Black undergraduate population, and it was essential to acknowledge that Black men and women experienced college differently (Nasir, McLaughlin, & Jones, 2009; Stewart, 2009; Wood & Palmer, 2015). Several scholars of the Black student experience throughout the literature highlighted the existence of a gendered difference (Cuyjet, 2006; Harper, 2005; Strayhorn, 2009; Wood & Palmer, 2015). There was a substantive amount of knowledge about and in support of Black men's needs: it focused on their disproportionately low college attendance compared to Black women and other ethnic groups, assumptions people made about their qualifications for attendance, and their involvement in student organizations as connected to Black men's development (Brown, 2019; Cuyjet, 2006; Harper & Quaye, 2007). There was also research about the intentional student development resources available to students via Black male brotherhood organizations meant to help Black men demonstrate citizenship, exhibit "values-based leadership," and connect members with supportive campus resources (Bledsoe & Rome, 2006).

Over the last several years, increasing research has focused on Black undergraduate women, addressing the importance of examining their experiences independently from their male peers, their distinctive position on campus, and their within-group differences (Patton, 2022; Patton & Croom, 2017; Winkle-Wagner, 2009; Banks, 2009; West, Donovan, & Roemer, 2009; Winkle-Wagner et al., 2019). Scholars asserted that Black women were not a monolithic group, and their contexts and social identities and experiences varied and deserved attention (Porter et al., 2020). It follows that the high-achieving students among them also deserved more consideration (Pearson & Kohl, 2010; Davis, 2018).

In one critical ethnographic study, Winkle-Wagner examined how identity was imposed on Black women in college and proposed a new sociologically based approach to considering this group of students' development (Winkle-Wagner, 2009). Findings from this study were consistent with the literature about Black students' experiences with racism as a group and the individual impact of an unwelcoming campus community. Women in the study responded to race-related stress by intentionally performing their race in a manner opposite the stereotypes they face in the classroom and leaning on campus resource programs for "financial, academic, emotional and social support" (Winkle-Wagner, 2009, p. 73). The findings also contributed to the knowledge on Black women's sense of identity. The students described feeling the "dueling" pressures of being in the "spotlight" or invisible in the classroom, of constantly representing themselves or their entire racial group, and needing to navigate the expectations of "good womanhood" versus being a good student. They struggled to control their "attitudes" among White peers and expressions of their "smartness" around other Black peers in order to fit in (Winkle-Wagner, 2009, p. 132). Of particular note was the way "race was gendered, and gender was racialized": students could not separate the influences of gender and race in their lives (Winkle-Wagner, 2009, p. 24). Many of the issues addressed in Winkle-Wagner's research persisted and were common among the academically talented Black women in my research.

Other contributions to the research on Black women addressed how they made meaning of their experiences and identity development (Porter, 2017), as well as cultural capital and university life (Banks, 2009; Commodore, Baker, & Arroyo, 2018; Patton & Croom, 2017). In their recent edited volume on Black women and girls, Patton, Evans-Winters, and Jacobs (2022) offered a collection of essays that share the experiences of Black girls and women in educational settings and offer important recommendations for enhancing their success in a variety of realms. An analysis of their participation in STEM initiatives (Joseph, 2022) and their involvement with school discipline and its connection with university life (Steele, 2022) offered fresh perspectives. One study highlighted a group of women's reflections on their choice to attend college and pathways and motivations they used to get them there (Patton, Copridge, & Sharp, 2022). Another employed a critical discourse analysis of the literature to highlight the importance of mental wellness and other psychological concerns affecting Black women undergraduates (Byrd & Porter, 2022). The innovative ways digital communities such as podcasts and social media discussions were used apart from institutional support were also analyzed, highlighting the ways peer support and accountability were offered by a virtual collective of Black women in higher education unbound by campus proximity (Robinson & Williams, 2022).

In their addition to the literature, Commodore, Baker and Arroyo (2018) highlight several issues facing Black women at college. Social homogeneity, isolation, lack of good mentoring relationships, mental health stress, and affording college were among the challenges for Black women highlighted in their guide to student success. Patton and Croom's (2017) edited volume on Black women and college success also addressed part of the research gap. Some of the leading and emerging scholars in higher education research on Black women provided a historical and generational perspective of Black women (Stewart, 2017), examination of identity politics (Porter, 2017), and strategies for institutionalizing support for Black women undergraduates (Shaw, 2017). Only one of the chapters focused on high-achievers: it examined the experiences of working-class Black women attending an Ivy League university (Johnson, 2017). This book contributed to the field by addressing the gender and the high-achievement gap in higher education research.

The complex identities of Black women required more attention in the research to address the inequality that hindered their college success. In order to succeed at PWIs, Black undergraduates must arrive with or learn strategies to manage the race-related stress caused by the individual and institutional challenges they face in that environment (Commodore, Baker, & Arroyo, 2018; Hoggard, Byrd, & Sellers, 2012; Chwalisz & Greer, 2007). Despite the obstacles they faced, the literature indicated that a number of these students were successful, which was a reflection of their strength and resourcefulness (Commodore, Baker, & Arroyo, 2018; Solórzano, Ceja, & Yosso, 2000). The ways these students persevered in the midst of the challenges they faced deserved attention too. Their success should be a product of their own agency as well as tailored community and institutional support.

The fact that racial identity impacted how Black undergraduates perceived and responded to the challenges they faced in college was well established in the literature (Jerald et al., 2017; Sellers, Chavous, & Cooke, 1998; Williams, 1998). And there was more nuance to understanding how Black students perceived their identities than noting how they negotiated "matters of race and the place of race in their self-concepts, meaning-making, and relationships with others," as Stewart argued (2009, p. 268). One essential contribution to the research on the importance of racial identity on students' experiences employed the Multidimensional Model of Racial Identity (MMRI), a psychosocial model that argued that racial centrality moderated an individual's understanding of how race impacted their life experiences and interactions with others (Sellers, Chavous, & Cooke, 1998). Racial centrality and racial ideology were two of the four dimensions of racial identity examined by the MMRI. Racial centrality was an indicator of how important race was to an individual's self-concept or the way someone generally defines themselves. This did not refer to an individual's understanding of what it meant to be Black (racial ideology), but instead, how central Blackness was to their self-definition. Sellers asserted that nuanced difference was unarticulated in some of the racial identity research, which conflated racial ideology with centrality.

Another significant contribution to the knowledge on racial identity was Porter's (2017) Model of Identity Development in Black Undergraduate Women (MIDBUW) based on a study on thirteen students attending a PWI. In the extended revision of the identity model, Porter's work affirmed that there were intersections in Black women undergraduates' identities and "illuminated the processes of one's articulation of identity through precollegiate and collegiate socialization, as influenced by personal foundations, media, role modeling, and while holding identities and interactions with others as constants" (Porter et al., 2020, p. 256). Porter's work addressed a gap in the research and established a link between socialization and identity development processes for college Black women.

The salience of race played a role in how students were affected by racist experiences (Jerald et al., 2017; Aronson & Inzlicht, 2004; Solórzano, Ceja, & Yosso, 2000; Yip, Seaton, & Sellers, 2006). For young Black women, a strong connection with their racial identity intensified the prevalence of anxiety and depression associated with the awareness of harmful stereotypes people had about them (Jerald et al., 2017). Racial salience also influenced how students defined their cultural identity (Carter, 2006), assumptions others made about their potential for academic success (Fordham & Ogbu, 1986), and how students themselves perceived the significance of their own achievement (Sanders, 1997).

One study of Black high school students' perceptions about racism and discrimination found that students' awareness of discrimination and their commitment to defying the stereotypes associated with their race fueled their motivation for achievement (Sanders, 1997). Students in that study used their strong sense of racial pride to achieve despite the anticipated obstacles associated with their race. The importance of race to the students' personal identity made them want to prove their abilities as equal to other groups by outperforming them.

There was also a complex relationship between racial identity and perceptions of racial discrimination. Sellers and Shelton found that racial centrality was positively associated with how often individuals detected discriminatory experiences, and perceptions of racial discrimination were associated with psychological distress. They also theorized that students might be more targeted for discrimination if others perceived they strongly associated with their race. Perceived racial discrimination harmed Black individuals immediately and over time in the form of anger, depression, low life satisfaction, intrusion, and avoidance of others (Sellers & Shelton, 2003, p. 1089). At PWIs like my research sites, where high-achieving Black women were outnumbered and often challenged about their belonging, these effects could be devastatingly harmful to their psychological wellbeing.

Environmental factors played a role in individual and group experiences associated with race as well. Students' racial identities were created from social forces from the institutional, group, and individual levels; they were complex and could shift as their meanings did in their manifestations in universities, communities, and among groups of people. Social practices within an environment could reflect how particular racial groups were accepted in their schooling environment (Carter, 2006, p. 307). In their study on constructions of race and academic identity in an urban public high school, Nasir, McLaughlin, and Jones found that local and distal context shape the way racial and academic identities were developed on the individual and group level. Expression of these identities was based on students' participation in school and community contexts and the "norms, conventions, and available roles within cultural practices in these institutional settings" (Nasir, McLaughlin, & Jones, 2009, p. 101). In a relatively homogenous racial setting, students were prevented from needing to "straddle culturally" across racial groups as part of their identity expression, but for high-achieving Black undergraduates at PWIs, it was an expectation.

Other studies focused on racial climate for Black students found that a negative racial climate and the racial microaggressions that occurred on campus had a harmful impact on students' academic and social lives (Jerald et al., 2017; Solórzano, Ceja, & Yasso, 2000). The prevalence of racist situations encountered by participants in the study indicated that, although some campuses could give the impression of equality, they were not in fact race-neutral and not all members of the campus community were welcome (Solórzano, Ceja, & Yasso, 2000, p. 71). The racialized, gendered, and academic setting of the university reinforced the systems of power in society that functioned to maintain Black people's subordination at the individual and institutional levels. As many of the aforementioned studies illustrate, racial identity alone could not explain all of the impact or impressions of Black undergraduates' experience (Sellers, Chavous, &

Cooke, 1998), particularly for high-achieving Black women undergraduates.

The way race was performed by Black women undergraduates was different from Black men's performances. Similarly, the ways White women embodied their gender was different from Black women's; expectations from society and interpersonal interactions pressured Black women to perform in a different way than their White peers. There was more than just sexism and patriarchy at play for Black women. There were particular norms and expectations ascribed to women in this group unique from other people in society.

Recent research addressed the overlaps in gender and racial identities and the role of structural issues. In their grounded theoretical study of Black women's identity development, Porter and Dean found that, for Black women, gender did not operate apart from race in experiences at college. Those identities were intertwined. They argued that "students often feel forced by systems and organizational structures to 'pick' a primary identity. African American women show up, exist, and survive through the lens of being both African American and female at the same time" (Porter & Dean, 2015, p. 136). Winkle-Wagner's study of African American young women also shed light on the gendered challenges faced by women in this population: "Because of their racialized (perhaps even unchosen) category as African American or Black, the women [in her study] encountered particular gendered prescriptions that were intended solely for them based on their race and gender categories simultaneously. Hence, gender was ultimately unchosen in many of the same ways as race . . . raced and gendered tug-of-war" (2009, p. 132). Earlier studies on the experiences of Black undergraduate women also noted this complex relationship between gender and race, further arguing that the "educational, social, and political positions of African American women in postsecondary education" needed more attention (Zamani, 2003). People existing at the intersection of both identity groups could not remove aspects of one identity to embody the other on its own.

The literature suggested that students had an awareness of how the systems of power in society present obstacles in relation to those identities. As one adolescent shared in an early study, "I know that being Black and being a woman, I am going to have to work harder to prove what I can do and what I can be" (Sanders, 1997). A student in my study echoed those sentiments. It was an unfortunate reality that these women faced challenges based on aspects of their identity that they cannot control or change.

Performing Academic Identity

There was value in acknowledging the intersectionality of participants' multifaceted identities, and there remained value in understanding how talented Black women viewed the importance of their academic performance and identifiers in particular. Students developed their sense of academic identity based on the norms and expectations in their environments, as with their other identities. One study found a predictive positive relationship for students with high ethnic identity and high academic achievement (Nasir, McLaughlin, & Jones, 2009). The complex meanings that African American high school students attributed to their academic identity were informed by the attitudes and practices in their school context (Nasir, McLaughlin, & Jones, 2009). Some researchers argued that peer groups could create a stigma against academic achievement among Black students because of its association with whiteness (Fordham & Ogbu, 1986). Often high-achievers or students that identified strongly with their academic identity endured accusations of "acting White" by their same race peers, an insult meant to criticize their association with one of their social identities based on cultural behavioral norms (Durkee et al., 2019; Ogbu, 2004; Carter, 2006).

In Carter's study on the experiences of performance of whiteness, students associated it with four aspects of behavior: verbal expressions by the group and its members; definition of boundaries for the group based on attire, style, and other mannerisms; and the nature of association with other people in their ethnic group. A number of contemporary researchers' examinations of the "acting White" phenomenon argued instead that some Black students' resistance to doing well in school was more of a resistance to White normalcy than it was a resistance to getting good grades or valuing education (Durkee et al., 2019; Winkle-Wagner, 2009; Spencer et al., 2001).

Portrayals of Black people in the media and popular culture, and the cultural and social norms where they live and learn, also produced numerous stereotypes associated with Black academic identity. There could be pressure socially to represent a particular kind of Blackness commonly associated with "speaking stupid" (Carter, 2006) or having an attitude. These stereotypes reflected a social perception that "producing intellectual work is generally not attributed to Black women artists and political activists. Such women were typically thought of as nonintellectual and non-scholarly, classifications that created a false dichotomy between scholarship and activism, between thinking and doing" (Collins, 1991, p. 15). Instead of simply studying or reading for class like their White peers, Black students had the additional pressure of validating their credibility in the classroom. The additional expense of psychological and emotional energy required to be prepared to defend their intellectual ability or other salient aspects of their identity could take a toll on students' academic self-confidence and hinder their performance

(Solórzano, Ceja, & Yosso, 2000; Fries-Britt & Turner, 2001; Jerald et al., 2017). The effort Black women expended combating stereotypes could instead be positively channeled into academic and social engagement (Harris-Perry, 2011; Winkle-Wagner et al., 2019). Their White peers did not exhaust their energy in such ways.

Especially at PWIs, where Black women students were underrepresented, there were also few faculty and staff who looked like them. In fall 2018 only 3 percent of all full-time faculty were Black women (40 percent were White men); only 2 percent of full-time professors (compared to 53 percent White men) and 5 percent of assistant professors (compared to 39 percent White females) at all degree-granting postsecondary institutions (National Center for Education Statistics, 2020). The presence of higher education administrators of color has grown, but it has not kept up with the attendance of students of color at college (Bichsel & McChesney, 2017, as cited in Commodore et al., 2018).

The idea of the smart Black woman ran counter to the pervasive representations undergraduate Black women face in reality; navigating their lives along the margins of the academic and social spaces at PWIs could have lasting effects on their emotional and psychological well-being. Racial, gender, and academic identity (individually and in combination) influenced how high-achieving Black undergraduate women make meaning around their experiences individually and as a group. Identity also played a role in understanding their place on campus and in society as people at the intersections of multiple systems of power. Taken alone or in binaries, race or gender or academic identity only explained a fraction of this population's positionality on campus or in greater society.

The criteria for the definition of high-achieving undergraduates remained problematic, both in practice and in the literature. Few studies examined the experiences of high-achieving students at the undergraduate level. Even fewer discussed the Black women among them. And while the research on high-achieving adolescents was becoming less obscure, much of the work focused on identifying or supporting talented students in K-12 schooling and failed to consider postsecondary experiences. Primary and secondary school programs used aptitude and IQ testing to evaluate students' intellectual ability, often placing talented students in special resource groups away from their peers or giving them access to unique academic or extracurricular resources, such as art or music programs.

A range of qualifications were used to identify high-achieving students at the university level. As college applicants, they had high SAT/ACT scores and excellent high school grades that often earned them merit awards and admission to an honors or scholars program in college. They may have also taken numerous Advanced Placement (AP), honors, and dual enrollment courses or participated in an International Baccalaureate program. Admission to honors communities varied by university; so precollege indicators may also have included student involvement in high school or a letter of recommendation from a teacher or a general application process that evaluated students' writing and critical thinking skills. Universities considered students that met these criteria to have potential for achieving academically and professionally (Fries-Britt & Griffin, 2007).

As matriculated college students, high-achievers were identified by the literature as having at least a 3.0 college GPA, high IQs, and membership in a scholars or university honors program (Freeman, 1999; Griffin, 2006; Harper & Quaye, 2007; Strayhorn, 2009); in Griffin's study of high-achievers' motivation, all of the participants were affiliated with the honors program at the university (Griffin, 2006).

Another study focused on the academic achievement and psychological pressure of a group of merit scholars (Strayhorn, 2009). There was consistency within the field on the kinds of qualifications for high-achievers, but those identifiers reinforced exclusivity (Davis, 2018; Borland, 2004). A review of the National Collegiate Honors Council member institution websites suggested that honors admissions qualifications vary by institution, but many screened participants based on scholastic achievement in high school, standardized test scores, or an application that requested information about students' community or extracurricular involvement.

Standardized tests continued to be a problematic admissions tool for honors, especially for students of color. Underrepresented students have historically had lower scores on the SAT than their White peers (Anderson, 2019; "More Blacks," 2008). College Board data from 2019 indicated that students with lower incomes and whose parents never attended college tended to score lower than their more privileged peers. More Black, Latinx and Native American students chose to take the test in recent years, which suggested that more were also considering college attendance. However, the fact that White and Asian students were almost twice as successful reinforced the perception that the SAT was wrought with class, cultural, and racial hurdles that obstructed minority student access to selective institutions (Anderson, 2019). AP exams also reflected racial differences in performance: less than one-third of Black students earned a 3 or higher on their exams in 2015, the lowest among all racial groups (Jaschik, 2015). As many universities require at least a score of 3, a limited number of students of color who have access to the courses even earn college credit for them. The lack of scholastic opportunities to take AP courses in preparation for high-stakes tests ("More Blacks," 2008) coupled with the criteria used to identify high-achievement status result in many talented and otherwise qualified young Black women being overlooked for academic opportunities (Borland, 2004).

In their study of high-achievers, Harper and Quaye used an inclusive approach, labeling high-achievers based on students' college GPA, campus leadership and involvement, connections with faculty and staff, engagement in academic enrichment opportunities (such as research programs and internships), and awards (Harper & Quaye, 2007)—a more holistic approach than using academic standards alone. High-achievement ability should not be characterized solely by students' performance in the classroom. Social involvement and demonstrations of character were also important factors in a student's ability to achieve, particularly when seeking to include historically underrepresented populations at PWIs.

As a practitioner of honors education, I observed that accepted characterizations of honors students did not always provide a model that fit high-achieving Black women college students, and this limitation was evident when considering the number of Black women served by honors programs. A quick review of well-known honors college websites revealed that statistics about race are commonly omitted from public information. At the time I did the study, only about 3 percent of the honors population were Black women at our urban PWI, a far smaller proportion than the institution at large, which had about 8 percent full-time undergraduate Black women. As intellectual and ethnic minorities at PWIs, Black women high-achievers were almost invisible.

Intersectional Identities

I grounded my design of this project, data collection, and analysis in intersectionality, using it as a lens through which to understand the experiences of the talented Black women undergraduates I centered in this project. I researched with the understanding that the mutual influence of race, age, gender, and class—among other identities—made the experience of Black women high-achieving undergraduates unique and meant they face complex social inequities (Collins, 2015). As Collins (1991) argued, "Black women's concrete experiences as members of specific race, class, and gender groups as well as [our] concrete historical situations necessarily play significant roles in our perspectives on the world" (p. 33). As undergraduates, their Blackness and womanhood made their educational journeys specific to them because of those and other intersecting social classes and locations in society (Banks, 2009). People embody more than one single isolated part of their identity—particularly Black women who were centered in this framework from a Black feminist standpoint. They were complex social actors whose backgrounds and perceptions played a role in how they experienced the world and how others perceived and responded to them. Intersectional theory supported this idea of identities as "always in the process of creating and being related by dynamics of power," which fostered the consideration of the various layers of identity of individuals and groups in various contexts (Cho, Crenshaw, & McCall, 2013, p. 759; Collins, 2012). I took the stance in my research that Black women undergraduates were "intellectual authorities" on their own experiences (Banks, 2009). By utilizing an intersectional framework to understand this population, my work examined how the interactions of their multifaceted identities and their oppressed positions within a system of power played a role in the challenges they faced inside and outside the classroom.

In its diverse intellectual iterations, intersectionality "helps reveal how power works in diffuse and differentiated ways through the creation and deployment of overlapping identity categories" (Cho, Crenshaw, & McCall, 2013, p. 797). This multilayered examination was what enabled intersectionality to address social problems in a way that traditional methods could not (Hancock, 2007). Three tools used to examine how power worked through overlapping identities include structural, political, and representational intersectionality (Crenshaw, 1991). Structural intersectionality referred to how the intersecting identities of Black women—such as race, gender, and class—made their experiences different from others that shared aspects of those identities; the lack of consideration of those differences in the law and other social policies meant to support them as members of different racial or gender groups often limited the availability of resources to this population.

Political intersectionality examined the importance of "inequalities and their intersections to political strategies" (Jordan-Zachery, 2007). More specifically, it addressed the problem that Black women occupy a space in oppressed groups that had rivaling political focuses—namely people of color versus women (Crenshaw, 1991). Antiracist arguments often neglected the issue of patriarchy, omitting the concerns of Black people who were also women; feminism lacked consideration of the discrimination faced by women who were also Black. As a result, Black women remained disempowered on both fronts (Crenshaw, 1991, p. 1241). Political intersectionality connected theory to practice by offering a method of resisting power through political and social action (Cho, Crenshaw, & McCall, 2013).

Representational intersectionality referred to the "cultural construction" of Black women in society (Crenshaw, 1991, p. 1245). Analyses of this nature focused on how the reproduction of gender and racial hierarchy fostered particular images of Black women that marginalize them, such as the mammy and Jezebel (Crenshaw, 1991). More recently, Black women were portrayed as "superwomen," who were expected to be strong and provide for others, even to their own detriment (Lewis et al., 2012; West, Donovan, & Daniel, 2016; Porter, 2017). And the #BlackGirlMagic idea used to empower Black women in their achievements also had the power to undermine how the realities of multiple oppressions impact and stifled that achievement (Patton, 2022). Intersectionality could be used as a tool to address how these particular images of Black women subordinated Black women racially, sexually, and by gender and were reflective of the intersecting power relations that affected them because of their social location.

Researchers in a number of disciplines incorporated intersectionality into their examination of social issues. My approach to intersectionality was informed by the six assumptions outlined by Hancock (2007), which included that more than one facet of a group or individual's identity was involved in analyzing social political issues. Although each of the identity facets matters individually and should be addressed, examining them together (instead of each in isolation) produced a richer illustration of the individual or group experience because of the influence of each facet on the other. In addition, identity facets manifested and contested at the micro—and macro—levels of society and studies should therefore impel discussion of how multifaceted identities interacted with political or social issues at those levels (Harper & Quaye, 2007). Hancock also included that there was heterogeneity among individuals within identity groups that should be considered in the development of any solutions to political issues and that, as an empirical and analytical framework, intersectionality should be used to guide the theoretical approach and may use multiple methods to address an issue (2007, p. 251). My work moved the work of intersectional analysis forward and also addressed the limitations and common critiques of this approach by considering how systems of power play a role in high-achieving Black undergraduate women's individual experiences, as well as the way this reflected their position in the university and greater society.

The literature made clear that exploring one identity alone could not fully illustrate the significance of the experiences of the talented Black undergraduate women I studied. In response, my research attentively examined the mutual influences of gender, race, academic, and other identities of the students whose experiences I brought to light. My research addressed how high-achieving Black women perceived their gender—in relation to and among other identities—in campus life to determine its importance in their experiences. My results found that high-achieving Black undergraduate women felt some of the same pressures to achieve and an awareness of the implications of their social identities in society and on campus as some of the students in prior research. I also elucidated several challenges unique to students in honors. Although identity centrality varied among students, awareness of the potential influence of these identities was essential to the development of supports that effectively meet the needs of this population on college campuses. May my intention to give voice to the challenges, triumphs, and meaning-making in college life of these talented Black women lead to the development of dynamic supports rooted in their needs.

~ 3 ~

Learning while Black and Brilliant

"The classroom remains the most radical space of possibility."
—bell hooks

Learning in the classroom signified more than the academic content in the syllabus for the smart Black women in this book. Whiteboards, desks, a lectern, and a projector were all fixtures of the college classroom. An instructor positioned at the front of a room, writing formulas on the board or sitting on the table discussing concepts with their students. Classrooms were the site of academic learning, the space where all students went to soak up information from faculty in their areas of expertise, where they were tested on their knowledge, where they got to know classmates who might become friends. Classrooms and other academic spaces could also be the site of challenging or supportive interactions with faculty and peers, and places where academically talented Black women continually proved themselves, where the threat of stereotypes loomed, a place where students can feel othered or welcomed, brilliant or unsure. Instructors had the power to shape the way discussion and other interactions were supported or discouraged. And as Jada's story illustrates, the classroom was where students learned if their voices would be valued or ignored.

For many Black women high-achievers, those rooms filled with faces that didn't resemble their own signified more than just where learning should happen. Classroom interactions with faculty and peers at PWIs offered memorable experiences—constructive and harmful—for this group of students. Based on these students' stories about traumatizing events in their classrooms, it was clear that faculty needed development to ensure discussions of race and other topics associated with students' marginalized identities did not alienate or draw undesirable attention to the talented Black women in their classes.

The academically talented Black women in this study placed high value on their relationships with their instructors, whether or not their connections with them felt constructive. In the interviews, some participants expressed a sense of feeling supported and welcomed in their classes or by their academic departments, but many acknowledged the significant trials they faced in the classroom that left them feeling scrutinized.

Despite their status as high-achievers, the Black women shared that they were often deliberate and measured with their class participation. Stereotypical high-achiever behavior assumed these students would be raising their hands and avid contributors in class. Answering questions and discussing the reading were some of the active learning and engagement behaviors that signaled to instructors that students were attentive and prepared for class. It was common practice for instructors to include participation as part of the grade for a course. But sometimes this group of students avoided contributing their voices because of a lack of self-assurance or their concerns about content mastery. Their confidence and their grades were at stake when they made choices about speaking up in class.

Shantel admitted that she listened actively in class but hesitated to raise her hand to add to the discussion. "I've always kind of had an issue with speaking in front of people," she confessed. Her affect and body language during her interviews were indicative of such behavior: her slouched posture and avoidance of eye contact came across as unsure and fairly tentative. In our conversation, she measuredly shared her opinions in a tone that seemed awaiting of my approval of her responses. Mia also painted herself as timid in the classroom, choosing not to speak up often and very much aware that she was the "token Black girl" in most of her classes, especially as a nursing major. Aisha was working on being less introverted; despite feeling fine meeting with professors during office hours, she "just can't bring [herself] to just openly just speak in class." Similarly, Anissa indicated she often hesitated to speak up, although she often found she knew the correct answer to questions. "I'm very quiet in class, so I don't like to answer questions. Like I'll say the answer in my head, and then someone will raise their hand, and I'll say, 'Wow, I got it right.'" Despite having a solid grasp on the material, she felt intimidated by her smart peers in the classroom.

Other times there were barriers that impeded even the most confident and outspoken students from contributing in the classroom. Students mentioned a fear that their thoughts would be dismissed or that their comments in discussions would be used as if they defined everyone who shared their identities. Lauryn was confident and generally outspoken, but in her required diversity course she often kept her opinions to herself. She tried to talk to her instructor but kept reflecting on her first impression of him. "At the beginning of the course, he told us he didn't really care about our opinions. So sometimes I didn't really say anything because he obviously didn't, like he really believes in his theory." The instructor positioned himself as the all-knowing authority for his classroom, discouraging students from engaging with him, and perhaps each other, preventing opportunities for debate.

Crystal's professor left little room for students' verbal contributions either. In one of her large general education courses, Crystal's professor often asked for class participation but tended to dominate the air space with his own voice. Instead of speaking up, she sat in the back of the room, listened to the lecture, and completed her assignments. With so many people in the class, there were too many students to get to know them all, especially a student like Crystal who did not speak up.

Amber also chose not to participate in class. Before the semester started, she was looking forward to taking her required diversity course and having an opportunity to "interact with other people on their ideas about race." Her actual experience with the course turned out to be very different from what she expected. Her professor did not welcome discussion. She also found the course material offensive. One day in class, the instructor played a video of a Dave Chappelle skit that included a blind Black man who had been raised by a White family to hate Black people. The professor gave no introduction to the sketch. Amber remembered, "And she played the movie and just kind of like went to the back and just sat there. And I remember everyone laughing and thinking the video was funny. And it just didn't sit right with me. I don't know. It was just not comfortable. That was a really uncomfortable moment for me. It was just really surprising. We didn't talk about it as a class. She just played it, and then went to the next video. And it was always something that was weird to me. So I was very aware I was Black in that moment." In a course focused on enhancing students' understanding and appreciation of diversity, the instructor's failure to engage students in conversations, particularly around such provocative material, made the environment uncomfortable.

In the examples above, the instructor's teaching style and approach to student interactions failed to produce a welcoming and inviting classroom environment. The participants described their professors' behavior as alienating, especially for students who felt more comfortable engaging material with their instructor one to one instead of in a formal classroom discussion, like many of those in the study.

Spotlighting

Another challenge Black women high-achievers faced in academic spaces was the negative, unwanted attention to their voices, bodies, or experiences as members of their social groups. Spotlighting led to an expectation that students under the microscope should be the representative for their identity groups and the default educator for their majority others. Their spotlighting commonly occurred during discussions of race. All thirteen of the students at Atlantic University alluded to a spotlighting situation in the classroom, even the first-year students.

Professors and students alike had a role in spotlighting the participants in the study. Anissa felt that her instructors "narrow in on me, and they're like, 'Okay, this girl, maybe she actually *is* really smart.'" She was self-conscious and sensed judgement from her professors based on the way she looked and how she stood out in her classroom as the only Black person. Because of this attention and her sense of how the instructors viewed her, she felt she had to "prove myself in a way. So that's why I study so hard for my tests: because I want them to know I'm much more than just what they see." She wanted her academic performance to be why her instructors paid her attention, not her skin color.

Jacqueline described a testy situation in one of her required honors humanities courses. As in many of her other honors classes, she was the only Black woman in the classroom. She acknowledged that her instructor was well intentioned with his solicitation of a variety of student voices into class discussions. When he put her on the spot as the default expert on Black life in the classroom, she felt he squandered an opportunity to make the assigned readings on African American experiences constructive for everyone, herself included. Although Jacqueline sometimes felt inclined to share her experiences to add a different perspective to discussions, this unwanted attention by her professor made her feel uncomfortable.

Aisha and Mia had similar experiences in their required humanities course. One day, the instructor began the class with a broad question: "What is an African American and how do you describe that?" The question was completely unrelated to the class texts. Every one of their classmates turned to look at Mia and Aisha at their end of the long conference table, waiting for them to respond. They remained silent. Their classmates kept staring. Imagine yourself in their seats, resisting all of their eyes coaxing you to speak. That tense situation in Aisha and Mia's classroom exposed the precarious dynamic that peers and faculty could create in classroom contexts.

Classmates actively spotlighted their Black women peers, giving them unwanted negative attention in class related to some aspect of their identity. Often participants were expected to be the spokesperson for their entire racial communities. Keshia was a sophomore health professions student at Atlantic University. In Keshia's experience, "When there's topics that come up with race or things, sometimes people look at me like I completely understand like the whole Black community, and I have no clue." Mia shared those sentiments. "I don't feel like I have to speak on behalf of the entire Black community, but people always expect me to. So that's kind of hard in the classroom." Miranda also felt the pressure of being under the microscope. "In the classroom, I often feel that when I speak up or disagree, my entire identity was under scrutiny. That's to say that I'm representing all people of color, or more specifically all women of color, with any comments I make." Classrooms should be spaces where dissent is welcome. Instead, classrooms were spaces where Black women students with smart ideas felt discouraged to contribute or the focus of unwanted attention. Neither helped these students succeed.

Even on topics outside of race, the study participants were scrutinized. As a student-athlete, Amber acknowledged her sensitivity to how people reacted to athletes on campus. To evade unwanted attention, she avoided wearing her athletic attire to class. After missing class for a student-athlete career development program, she approached her professor before class started to excuse her absence and learn more about what she missed from the lecture. Despite attempting to communicate with her instructor discreetly, "three people whipped their heads around and are like, 'Oh, you're a student-athlete!'" Their exclamations alerted everyone in the room to her hidden identity. Amber felt outed in that moment and consciously considered the ways she discussed her needs with faculty after that experience.

Anissa was also conscious of her classmates' scrutiny. Taking calculus in high school made her confident about her skills, but she found that her classmates seemed surprised by her abilities. "So it's interesting to see when I answer questions in calc class how people kind of like—you can see like this slight turn of a head," she said. She had the sense that her participation was unwelcome by her peers. She felt they judged her based on what she looked like without even knowing anything about her. After being spotlighted like this, students felt anger, frustration, self-doubt, and tokenized: emotional challenges their peers did not have to surmount. They also felt self-conscious about speaking up at all.

It was unproductive and unjust for high-achieving Black women to have to expend intellectual and emotional energy defending themselves from unwanted attention. The pressures that peers and professors placed on them inside the classroom were detrimental to learning. Black women were not at college for the purpose of informing others about their life experiences or as the representatives for their social groups, but their tokenized presence in the classroom situated them as the default educators for their peers and professors. Society groups Black women together based on skin color and assumptions about shared collective experience. In reality, individuals did not necessarily have common backgrounds and experiences reflective of their assumed racial or ethnic communities. Many of the participants acknowledged not feeling deeply immersed in the "Black experience" or what they sensed their racial majority peers assumed about them. As intersectional people with varying social class, family nationality, sexual orientation, and other identities, a number of the students struggled with how they fit in or not with how society expected them to perform as racialized beings. The pressures they felt in the classroom exacerbated those feelings.

To avoid being spotlighted or unwillingly being labeled the representative for their various identity communities, some academically talented Black women described themselves as hiding in plain sight in the classroom. For those who perceived the classroom as a hostile space, raising their hand drew even more unwanted attention and pressure. Some avoided the gaze of their peers by purposely exhibiting behaviors that made them less visible.

"I try to make myself invisible. . . . It just happens in some way," Shantel said. "I like to wear black . . . I have a lot of dark clothes. I mean, that doesn't necessarily make me invisible, but I feel like people avoid me then." Shantel did not want to draw any unnecessary attention to herself. Aisha avoided eye contact with her peers and instructors, particularly when she did not want to become the default contributor to conversations about race. The best way to avoid becoming the center of unwanted attention was to be unseen.

Some of the participants chose silence as an emotional defense mechanism. Jacqueline felt it was hard to recover the confidence to participate in class after being spotlighted. "It's hard, and I probably lost a lot of participation points in my humanities classes just because I couldn't figure out how to participate, especially after instances of such tension." She feared that the discomfort would repeat itself in other instances.

On more than one occasion, Miranda was on the receiving end of class discussion that objectified people of color. When she did choose to speak up about the sweeping generalizations her classmates made about the university's low-income neighborhood or other social issues, she felt that her opinions were not valued. Silence was safer. "I feel like if I really vocalized every single time someone said something in class, even a professor that was just questionable, I would be fighting a lot. And I don't mean fighting in the sense that

I'm being loud and being aggressive, but really just getting into arguments with people because of some of the things that they say. So sometimes for my own personal well-being, I have to just bite my tongue and say they don't know any better." Although she often felt defensive of her own community, she realized that it was not her job to serve as the representative to foster her peers' awareness. Silence was self-preservation.

Unfortunately, an unsupportive classroom was not a new phenomenon for a number of the participants, and issues with silencing and visibility were present in their high school learning environments as well. At her rural public high school, Miranda often felt that adding her voice to classroom discussion would "lack credibility" because she was not part of the dominant social or academic group of students whose voices were privileged in those spaces. They cut her off in class. They ignored her. Being dismissed by her peers led to academic self-doubt, preventing her from confidently contributing until her later years in school. "It was like anything I said, [when] I raised my hand, if it wasn't the smartest thing in the world it was immediately kinda just brushed off." Aisha and Keshia echoed this sentiment, citing similar situations in their small town high schools as well. Their experiences illustrated that the challenges high-achieving Black women faced in the classroom at college were endemic: the students had to overcome obstacles to success in their earlier academic experiences as well.

Jacqueline and Miranda's sentiments were an indicator that study participants were not avoiding participation out of lack of interest or knowledge. The hostility of their classroom environments reflected the systemic issues affecting their social groups in society. Their "choice" to not participate was an act of self-preservation within a system that limited their agency. And in the instances they chose to speak up despite those barriers, their participation was an act of resistance.

Participation in Class

As they strategically measured their participation, students chose other methods to assert their engagement with the material and send their instructors the message that they were engaged in the course. Despite her anxiety around participating in class discussions, Shantel tried to make it a point to let her professors "know that I'm engaged and that I'm listening and that I'm there." She stayed after class to talk with the professors with whom she felt more comfortable. Anissa was quiet in nature and preferred to connect with her faculty during office hours. Although she found it awkward and sometimes struggled to know what to do there, she would go ask questions so that they could get to know her.

Mia admitted that she tried to speak up sometimes. "But it takes me a while to build up the courage to raise my hand a lot. If I need something, if I have questions, then I'm comfortable going up to my professors after class and asking them or sending them an email if I need to." For Mia, the classroom environment posed the obstacle, not the communication with the instructor.

Black women high-achievers were intentional about ensuring their instructors knew that they were prepared for class and well versed in the material. Some participants valued these connections because of their intent to request references later in their academic careers, noting that if their instructors liked them and knew their names, they would be more apt to support their candidacy for future opportunities. Others simply went through the motions of performing the student behaviors that suggested they were engaged learners because they knew it would positively impact their grade. Regardless of their motivation or the challenging conditions they faced, maintaining a relationship with their instructors was important to them, whether they nurtured those connections during, after, or outside of class.

In the situations students described, questions or comments from faculty and peers made the classroom feel tense, hostile, and unwelcoming. Some professors were simply better at moderating discussion of sensitive topics than others. Likewise, students' skill level for constructively addressing those topics varied. Instead of being one individual student among a room of capable learners, smart Black women—who were already very sensitive to their minoritized status—were under scrutiny. Not all people of color or women or high-achieving students had the same experiences, but being the only one who looked like them in their classrooms certainly objectified them. Regardless of their classmates' and instructors' intention, unwanted critical attention could have an intense negative impact on how high-achieving Black women perceived the tone of their learning space.

Classroom Supports

Black women high-achievers did have constructive experiences to share. As discussed in the previous section, these students were particularly attentive to the nature of interactions with their faculty members. Despite the pressure she felt to perform in her highly competitive nursing program, Keshia made connections with a couple of her instructors early in her college career. She expressed her appreciation for one who had written her a letter of recommendation. The other, her clinical instructor, she described as a role model: like Keshia, she beat the odds to pursue higher education. Despite numerous obligations in her personal life, her clinical instructor had persevered to pursue her master's degree in nursing education and was modeling the way for her students to be successful. Keisha said, "I think it's nice to know them on a personal level, because they want us to succeed, as much as we don't think they do. But it just helps me to do better in classes. I can email them, like I don't understand something or that they can ask me, 'Can you tutor somebody?' or just something like that."

Shannon also had favorable impressions of her professors. As a senior STEM major at Polytech University, she recognized the importance of their relationships. "In the classroom, it's always a big deal for me to always make a really good impression on my professors," Shannon noted. As one of the only women and students of color in her White male–dominated STEM major, she felt that her ability to demonstrate to her instructors early on that she was "high-achieving and smart" helped ensure that she would be considered when opportunities arose. Her impressive resume, filled with internships, co-ops, and shadowing experience, offered strong support for her argument. "I've received emails, and it's so nice because they're like, 'This made me think of you. You should apply.' So in the context of the classroom, I really try to put forward my best foot; I try not to fall asleep in class; I try to be really good, like really get those good grades." Although she admitted to sometimes dozing off in one of her early classes, her close relationship with that instructor allowed her access to his network of colleagues and professional opportunities.

Anissa also felt the need to behave in a particular way to manage her professor's perception of her. Her instructor in one of her large science classes did not know her very well, but she felt pressure not to ever miss class because as the only Black person in her classroom, her absence would be obvious. She acknowledged the pressure to perform academically in a way that would not reflect poorly on her or others that look like her.

Serena had a professor at Atlantic University who encouraged her and took an interest in fostering her academic achievement in her course. For one of her papers in her required diversity course, she reflected on her identities as Nigerian American and Black and woman and found that the professor took an interest in her experiences. "So, she was always kind. She always talked to me about things like this and always wanted me to expand on that ... she would give me materials on this and [kind of] we would always talk back and forth about the issues that I brought up in that paper." Her professor made her feel like her background and experiences mattered and helped make her experience in that particular classroom constructive and supportive.

Grace felt supported and welcomed and liked her professors. She generally described them as very knowledgeable and friendly. Since her major was a fairly small intellectual community at Polytech University, she anticipated she would get to know them quite well before graduating. She felt good about being able to approach them if she needed help with her coursework, but she was still shy about spending time in their office during office hours or talking to them outside of class.

Miranda felt that her professors were very good overall, particularly in her honors courses. "I have had nothing but good experiences with my upper levels. I feel like the professors are always great. They're small classes. People are engaged. We talk about real substantive issues, and no one's just trying to sound good. Everyone's genuinely trying to understand what's going on and learn from it. So those classmates, my honors classmates, are great."

Michelle was generally positive about her classroom experience. She felt that her honors peers provided "lots of different perspectives" in class. She was particularly happy about her instructor's diverse course readings in her diversity class.

The inclusion of works from multicultural authors on a variety of social issues was in stark contrast to Michelle's STEM major and other classes that touched on race. "In other classes I had where we talked about race, it was always an upper-class White person talking about how they perceived race. And a lot of these books were either written by . . . one was written by a Latin American woman, a couple were written by Black authors, and they gave a well-rounded understanding of how race is a very political thing in America and how it actually affects different kinds of people."

Black women high-achievers described their relationships with their instructors as a major part of their academic experience. When instructors and academic departments were supportive, it fostered positive learning environments. This finding reinforced the importance of student-faculty interactions (Pascarella, 1980; Umbach & Wawryznski, 2005), their varying impact based on students' gender and other identities (Sax, Byrant, & Harper, 2005), and the tone of campus learning environments for undergraduate Black women (Patton & Croom, 2017). Related research also examined the influence of sociocultural stressors like the ones the students in this study experienced (Donovan & Guillory, 2017) and analyzed how Black women were able to "struggle successfully" (Shaw, 2017).

Analysis of Classroom Experiences

Academic spaces posed both challenges and supports for academically talented Black women. Students shared that their individual interactions with faculty and smaller honors courses were mostly constructive and supportive academic experiences. In contrast, many classroom or academic contexts were not. Participants often depicted their classrooms as inhospitable. Spotlighting and other negative interactions in academic spaces posed a major threat to the success of high-achieving Black women in the classroom. For better or worse, students exercised self-preservation in the form of silence to successfully navigate those academic spaces.

Another problematic reality for many of these students was that their successful navigation of academic networks required them to subscribe to respectability politics. Students with the social capital to figure this out—like Shannon and Miranda described—thrived in these environments, clearing the hurdles before them. Students without those skills, or the network to support them through those challenges, may not have achieved their potential. Participants acknowledged the importance of making a favorable impression on their instructors and the professor's role in creating a safe space to engage with others or their reinforcement of a hostile environment. They also portrayed how their peers contributed to the insensitive tone of the learning environment.

Although some students had positive impressions to share about their academics, envision how successful Black women could be if they all felt free to be their authentic selves in the classroom. If they could raise their hands without fear and contribute to discussions without repressing parts of their identity. PWIs need to take action to enhance the sense of safety and belonging for this group of students to foster their retention, satisfaction, and enable them to reach their academic goals. It is a crisis that, despite their intellectual ability to excel in their courses, academically talented Black women are forced to struggle to succeed in the classroom by unjust learning conditions.

~ 4 ~

Thriving and Threats in Campus Life

Academically talented Black women spent their time outside the classroom like many other college students. They studied for class, spent time on social media, and watched Netflix. They explored their urban locale, went to concerts, and ate or relaxed with friends. Some were involved in a wide range of organized campus life activities. The stories they told about campus life were often positive and supportive, while in many other instances they acknowledged that interacting with their peers and where they spent their time was threatening. Participants in the study felt othered in some social spaces and found themselves serving as educators on "all things Black culture." They mentioned several microaggressions they experience from their peers. In contrast, participants also shared a number of constructive experiences from their social interactions, including making friends in their living environments, leadership opportunities, and surrounding themselves with people to support them.

Students described themselves as peer mentors, sorority members, admissions ambassadors, and dance troupe performers. They were singers, musicians, Christian youth fellowship members, and mentors for local school children. Black women high-achievers were also student leaders. Shannon and Nicole were organization presidents, while many were on the executive teams of their groups, and others were active members of organizations across their university. A few were involved in philanthropic and service groups, and a number of the students attended meetings for their professional or career affiliations.

Most of the students were in at least one group that reflected some aspect of their multifaceted identities, including ethnicity, race, academic major or excellence, gender, or political preference. Amber and Shannon participated in the Caribbean associations at their universities. Amber was also a Division I student-athlete. Aisha and Serena were part of the campus ministry, while Anissa attended a church near campus. Grace was in the choir and a music ensemble. Keshia, Miranda, and Shannon were sorority women. Mia, Michelle, and Zoe participated in service and philanthropy groups. Jacqueline, Lauryn, and Nicole committed their time to women's advocacy and empowerment groups. About two-thirds of the students were involved in preprofessional affiliation groups.

Only a handful of the students were in just one organization. Amber's athletic team commitments precluded her from participating in student activities regularly, but she enjoyed attending the Caribbean Association meetings and events when she was able. Crystal's involvement was also limited. She spent most of her time focused on studying, doing homework, or spending time with her boyfriend. She was only a member of the Association of Computer Machinery Women. She said she did not make friends easily. At the end of the semester she made some connections that she anticipated would help her get more involved the next year but felt she was generally disconnected from campus life. Both Amber and Crystal expressed the desire to be more involved, particularly in initiatives for students of color in honors, and generally in the campus community.

Shantel was not involved with any campus organizations and was the only participant without connections to student life. Shantel resided locally in her family's home and commuted to campus. Her demanding employment schedule that helped cover costs for college was an obstacle to her involvement. "If I'm not in class, I'm probably at work," Shantel said, with a shrug. "I pretty much work. . . ." She generally worked about twenty-three hours per week at a food truck near campus. "The way my schedule is, I have like an hour between class and work, and I usually just go right to work and talk to my co-workers and stuff." With her hours often conflicting with evening organization meetings, and needing to make time to study, Shantel did not have much extra time for social activities. She felt a stronger sense of community with her co-workers more than her campus.

Other employed students balanced working with hearty social involvement. Shannon worked during every year of college; in her senior year, while interning and taking fewer credits, she had two jobs. She worked on campus at Polytech University as a help desk assistant, which was a good fit for her future career in information technology. She also worked part time at a local coffee shop for about twenty hours per week. She was saving her money for a down payment on an apartment for the following year, when she would start her career in another city. Since her first year she was an active member of a women in science organization and her sorority, adding chapter president to her responsibilities in her senior year.

Nicole worked in the university student center for about fifteen hours per week. She was very active in campus life as well, serving as the president of the Black business student group and a member of a Black women's empowerment group at Atlantic University. She was also a mentee in an external organization for future industry leaders. Miranda waited tables on the weekends, saving money to help support herself while at school. She was also an active volunteer, peer mentor, and leader in her sorority and debate team.

Each of the employed participants, and those who did not have jobs, indicated that their parents or university scholarships covered much of the financial costs associated with their college attendance. Although Shantel, Nicole, Shannon, and Miranda needed to work in order to afford their college experience, each was proud of her ability to subsidize what her parents contributed. Miranda enjoyed being a server so that she could take her pay from each night and "pay for my utilities, my phone bill, my groceries, and transportation." Shannon was also able to fund most of her own nontuition expenses and did not ask her parents for money. She had a number of paid internships during college. "When I was working, I was getting paid enough that I never had to ask them for money," Shannon said. "I went abroad a couple times. They never had to pay for my flights or my lodging, nothing like that." With the exception of Shantel, working did not get in the way of their involvement in campus life; they managed to give time to both. Participating in community and campus organizations and working were common experiences among this group of talented black women.

Feeling Different outside the Classroom

At their PWIs, Black women high-achievers were often the only ones with their identities in social spaces, particularly their most visible identities. Although not all of the students felt constantly aware of their differences from their peers, most described situations when they felt sensitive to those differences. Michelle was aware of her racial difference from her peers in her professional organization. "When I look at the people in the org [also], there's not as many people that look like me. There's still some, which is nice, but I feel like I have to . . . I don't know. I feel like I'm representing all the other people, all the other Blacks or minorities in general, who want to be speech pathologists but aren't in the group or not here." Michelle sensed that she was the representative for her identity groups in that social space because there were so few like her. Miranda experienced being the only one on an organizational level. She was keenly aware of her team's othered status among the elite universities at tournaments for her debate league. Most teams were all White and male from private colleges, in contrast to Atlantic University, which was public and had a few minority members. When Atlantic first started in the league, "I think there were some barriers to entry, for some obvious reasons," Miranda said, alluding to the status and racial discrepancies. "It was really just tough for people and we had a low retention rate because people just didn't feel comfortable at tournaments. I've even talked to one of my friends here, Deepthi. She used to debate in high school, and she said the reason she doesn't do it now is because of those kinds of dynamics." Miranda and her friend described that environment as tiring. Deepthi chose not to continue, but Miranda stuck with it. "The debate is dominated by White men, and it was tiring, and she had no interest in doing it again," Miranda reasoned. "So we lose people a lot because of that." Feeling uncomfortably different was a common challenge for the participants.

In her predominantly White sport, Amber was the only Black athlete on her team. As the only one, she was sensitive to how others associated her abilities with her race instead of her talent. "So obviously there's a stigma, like I jump higher, blah, blah, blah, run faster—which I do," Amber said. "But, you know, there are things where it's like, I don't want that to just be the only reason why I am able to have that sort of athletic ability. I work just as hard as everyone else." Amber disliked that others assumed she only performed well on the court because she was Black. Not all Black people were naturally good athletes: she disliked being reduced to a stereotype.

Nicole was often the only Black woman in many of her social spaces, so she was particularly aware when she was not, and so were some of her White peers. She described a time when the presidents of some of the business organizations were all in the office at the same time, each representing a different background: one African American, one Chinese, one Middle Eastern, and one White American. "So he was like, 'I'm the only White guy in the room.' And me and this other [one] are like, 'Yeah, well like try being us. . . . This happens all the time.'" Nicole hoped that experience showed him how it felt to be the only one, but reasoned that "if I went around pointing that out all the time, ['cause it's like] I'd be saying it a lot, you know?" Outside of the multicultural community she created for herself and the multicultural groups she belongs to, it was different for the roles to be reversed.

Amber was also sensitive to the difference when she was not the only Black woman in campus spaces. Like many of the other participants, Amber was conscious of the lack of people who looked like her in her classes, so she was happy to see so many students of color emerge on her campus quad once the weather was nice. "You know the fraternities and sororities have events at the quad, and I go. And it's kinda like, where are all these Black women—and not just Black women, Black *people* on campus? I didn't know there were that many Black women that went to school here." For the participants who were not immersed in multicultural communities at college, encountering a concentration of students who shared their racial and gender identities was surprising. Crystal referred to that community as "Black Atlantic," suggesting that there was an underground group of students she did not know how to access. She described the quad emergence as if she missed the memo for all the Black students, unsure where to find others who looked like her until she made a connection with someone else who did. Crystal hoped her new roommates for the next year, other Black women she stumbled upon on Facebook, would help facilitate that connection.

Anissa also longed for that connection. Faced with the possibility of being the only person of color in most of the sorority houses she visited on rush night, she was concerned about whether she would find an organization that would make her feel comfortable and welcome. Anissa hoped to get connected with more Black women on campus at Polytech University. "But apparently they do have Black sororities. I don't know where, but apparently they do. So maybe I'll join one of those." As a freshman, she was in the process of figuring out where she fit in campus life. As her experience illustrated, being the only one mattered in her navigation of social spaces. On the other hand, because of the unique intersections of her cultural and racial identities in particular, she was concerned about navigating a community of all Black women as well. She said she hated to make it about race, but she would often "feel like I'm too Black for the White people and too White for [Black] people." Even among peers who shared some of her identities Anissa still felt like the only one.

The residence halls were a common space where students felt like "the only one." Crystal, Aisha, Mia, Serena, and Anissa all noticed they were among very few Black people in their hall, particularly on their floors or in the honors spaces. "I was the only Black person in my entire hallway, which I thought was like crazy," Crystal said. Coming from a high school where there were more Black people, at Atlantic she felt very isolated, disconnected, and "lonesome." Crystal also felt weird around the other Black honors students she did meet who went to high school where they were used to being the only one. "They don't feel why I'm uncomfortable [either]. So it's . . . it's a strange dynamic at Atlantic." The university and residential culture were uncomfortable.

Aisha and Mia also noticed they were the only Black women in their hall at Atlantic University. "I think there's only one other Black person in my hall. I just noticed that recently," Mia reflected. "I thought that was kind of weird." Serena recalled "maybe two other Black girls that I remember seeing around" when she lived on the honors floor but did not have any interactions with them. In the present year, she felt it was "cool finally having someone that had the same experience, well, similar experiences and similar struggles that I had" as her roommate. She was happy she had a roommate who shared more than just her gender and academic identities. She was also happy to be living on a more ethnically diverse floor, although she admitted her floormates mostly keep to themselves.

Living among honors students was a challenge and a support for Anissa. She appreciated that they were all focused on doing well in their academics; the problem was that her predominantly Indian hallmates ostracized her for spending time with other Black students instead of just them. One night while she was studying, she declined an invitation to hang out at an Indian fraternity house because she planned to spend time with other friends when she was done with her work. "And they're like, 'Oh, your *African* friends,'" which she felt obligated to reiterate was not the only reason they were friends. As the only Black woman in her friend group on her floor, she felt sensitive about how race mattered in her interactions with them. "I have friends from all different races, like why does it matter, you know?" In the place that should feel like a home away from home, many academically talented Black women felt othered.

MICROAGGRESSIONS

The sense that Black women high-achievers had that they were unwelcome in social contexts was undeniable: their peers made comments or gestures that elicited their concern. These microaggressions—both the threat of them and their occurrence—played a role in how students navigated campus life. A number of the participants who experienced these sometimes subtle putdowns or insults about their identities experienced similar critical comments in predominantly White schooling environments before attending college. But knowing the threat did not change the irritation nor insult the women felt about the gestures directed at them.

Some situations were minor concerns and easily disregarded, while others were more serious. Aisha shared about an experience with her campus ministry group during a potluck event. Her friends encouraged her to play some Nigerian music while they were socializing, so she approached the person managing the playlist. When she told him the song, he wanted to know what it was, and when she explained, he leaned over to his friend and audibly scoffed at her wanting to play Nigerian music. "I was like, 'Yeah, is that a problem?' . . . He played it anyway, but I just didn't know how to feel about that. It's just made me very self-conscious about me being Nigerian." In that particular interaction, Aisha's nationality was a sensitive identity in the context of her Christian community.

There were a number of situations that made students feel sensitive about their identity. Anissa's Indian friends from her floor pointed out every Black man they encountered on campus and called each of them her "future husband." Serena's friends made race jokes on occasion or insensitive comments about social issues that related to her identity groups. She was particularly bothered that a friend often commented that she's "so dark in the picture" when they would take group photos. Keshia's sorority sisters said they can "always remember your name, because you're one of the four Black girls," reducing her identity to the color of her skin.

In her freshman year, one of Jacqueline's White floormates in the honors hall would joke that he and their friends would "just take Jacqueline when we go out" so that they would be protected. He insinuated that she would help them look less out of place in their urban locale. Or maybe they expected her to aggressively protect them from the other Black people in the neighborhood. Her retort was that "I don't want to be your token Black friend, you know, keep you from getting shot by the locals." She was very upset by his comment and told him it was offensive. In a more injurious situation, the same friend also pressured Jacqueline into "saying something Black" one night at the residence hall. When she refused, he kept her from leaving the room. She locked herself in her friend's bathroom to avoid him, and eventually gave in, yelling, "F—k the police!" to be released. Out of caution and to prevent any other uncomfortable situations, she decided not to be friends with him anymore. That kind of traumatic experience could be emotionally scarring and negatively impact her willingness to make friends.

It was also common for people to touch the students' hair, or try to, without their consent. Sensitivity was relative about this issue, however. When trying to explain Black cultural practices to her peers, Jacqueline was alright with people touching her hair. Aisha was as well, noting that people were usually just curious. She had a friend from a small town whom she knew had never been near many people of color. So despite not wanting her to touch it, Aisha did not protest; she did remain sensitive to the gesture despite her inaction. "I'm a little bit insecure about my hair. So the whole curiousness about it and people just touching it and just asking questions about it, I'm like, can't we just pretend it's just hair, you know? Hair is hair. It's just the thing on my head. It's not something to just look at and observe, you know?" Students in the study cited hair as a common point of education with peers. The women felt they had to explain it to friends or acquaintances because they were innocently ignorant or very nice about their interest in learning more. But silently complying allowed others to violate their personal space and forced students to be the source of all information on Black hair. The students felt frustrated and objectified.

Thriving in Campus Life

In contrast to the challenges students faced in campus life, they also had a number of constructive experiences. Some study participants made social connections, did meaningful service, and developed a sense of community at college.

After only a few weeks on campus, Anissa felt very comfortable with her friends from the African Student Association. "I don't have to even pretend at all," Anissa said of her African friends. "I can just be myself, and I'm just there. They talk and it's like they're smart too, they know what I'm feeling, they know what we're going through. I have a commonality between them." She enjoyed the friend group she was building based on their common heritage. Anissa lived in the honors community with other freshmen and felt very close to them from the beginning as well, though they did not have common heritage. She and her friends from her floor frequented the dining hall together and encouraged each other to study. She liked that everyone was open to doing things with anyone on the floor and that they were not cliquish.

Michelle also felt connected to the members of the organizations she joined. The Black organization for community service at Atlantic University gave her opportunities to get to know other members. "I'm closest with the people in the [organization]. I feel like we do more as an org, I guess because we're smaller and hang out at the president's apartment or something like that. And when we go to community events like we'll all travel together." Bonding with her peers while giving back to the local community helped her build a network of close friends. Jacqueline and Miranda volunteered their time on campus as part of a peer mentoring program. They were trained to help first-year students navigate the transition to college, pick their courses, and find support resources.

Crystal belonged to only one organization: a professional association that provided opportunities for women in the computing field. Compared to her classes, she was one of many minority people at those gatherings. "Most of them are like Indian or Asian or things like that, so it, it's more inclusive and representative. So I, I just feel like [a] girl in the group rather than the Black girl in the group there, so I like it there." Crystal was especially impressed that the events offered by her college featured diverse voices. "You know, that never happens . . . but, unless it's a plan, planned thing. So not only were they women, but they were Black." She had grown accustomed to being the only one in so many spaces and was pleasantly surprised and excited about a recent "women in technology" panel discussion. "It was very insightful," Crystal added. "And I guess they were doing well, and the one girl, she was like, 'You'll be fine.'" Getting to see people who looked like her and being encouraged by them made Crystal feel more confident about her future professional plans.

Being in a sorority helped Shannon and Keshia "feel at home" at college. Shannon joined in her first semester at Polytech University and remained active in her chapter throughout college, becoming president in her senior year. Being a sorority woman provided her with leadership experience she felt would help her in her career. Keshia enjoyed cooking with her friends and trying new restaurants in their city. After joining her sorority at Atlantic University, Keshia noted she was "starting to feel at home with certain girls. And they're, I'm really, I could be myself with them." Connecting with other women was common in Crystal's, Shannon's, and Keshia's involvement in organized activities in campus life. For each of the students, finding the spaces on campus where they felt they shared common identities or academic or social interests helped them feel welcome and feel they could contribute to student life on campus. For Black undergraduate women, that sense of connection with a community could foster their retention, satisfaction, and ability to attain their goals at the university and beyond.

Analysis of Experiences

Analysis of the participants' experiences outside the classroom indicated that much of their time was spent in their living environment or in the context of student organization gatherings. Some optimistically reflected on their time in the halls, but many of the Black women high-achievers shared about the memorable trials they experienced in that context.

The microaggressions and othering they described drew attention to the ways systemic social issues manifested in campus life. Even in honors residential communities, the participants indicated consciously recognizing they were "the only one" and how that played a role in their perceptions of their living space as well as how others interacted with them.

In their organizations, being the only one was also a point of concern. To find a community among their predominantly White peers, the students associated themselves with groups that celebrated and acknowledged their identities. From nationality to gender, and identity groups in between, most of the students were immersed in campus life.

The narratives of the study participants illuminated some of the conditions that other students of color faced and that high-achieving undergraduate Black women who attend PWIs may encounter at their own universities. Existing research echoed these findings more broadly for students of color. Engaging with majority peers was challenging when interactions may be tinged with racism (Kanter et al., 2017; Swim et al., 2003; Solórzano, Ceja, & Yosso, 2000; Winkle-Wagner, 2009). Black women high-achievers felt unwelcome and isolated from their peers of color at college (Fries-Britt & Turner, 2001; Solórzano, Ceja, & Yosso, 2000; Commodore, Baker, & Arroyo, 2018; Winkle-Wagner et al., 2019). Their experiences were consistent with descriptions in extant research on students with similar identities.

Not all Black people had the same hair texture or skin tone. Not all Black people spoke like rap artists or came from rough neighborhoods. Despite having the opportunity to get to know them as people, peers chose to narrow smart Black women down to their race. It was racist to assume that all the Black people on campus knew each other or wanted to be in intimate relationships simply because of shared racial identity. All students deserved the opportunity to be their authentic selves without the threat of abuse from their peers. Academically talented Black women needed safer, more supportive campus environments.

Outside the classroom, in their places of residence, students often felt othered. Over time, microaggressions built up. Trying to develop in and contribute to an unsupportive social environment could make this group of students more sensitive about their identities and impact their well-being (Jerald et al., 2017; Byrd & Porter, 2022). The experiences of the study participants illustrated that, although high-achieving Black women gained access to the social spaces at their PWIs, in many cases they did not feel accepted within them. Students often sought community among those with similar backgrounds to help them navigate the rough waters of their PWI. Their experiences revealed how essential an engaged life outside the classroom was to the students' connection to their university and its community.

Without the option to remove themselves from hostile spaces or to avoid all of the threatening social interactions, academically talented Black women managed to persist toward their personal and professional goals despite those challenges. What were colleges doing to help these students remain successful? How were they helping them feel safe and welcome in campus life? These questions needed attention, and these students needed support.

~ 5 ~

Performing Authentic Identities

"We ask ourselves, 'Who am I to be brilliant, gorgeous, talented, fabulous?' Actually, who are you not to be?"
—Marianne Williamson

The smart Black women in the study were keenly aware of how much their complex identities mattered in the different contexts they navigated at college. The salience of the facets of who they were as well as their mutual interaction were essential to understanding how they made meaning. Although there were instances where the students felt particularly strongly about a single identity, overall their self-descriptions reinforced the often inextricable nature of their identities as people who lived at the intersections. Their distinctive overlapping identities produced a unique social position in society and in campus life.

It was essential to explore what it meant to have membership in the identity groups the students selected and why that mattered to them. A few students were able to describe the various aspects of those identities in separate pieces, noting situations when they felt particularly Black or intensely aware they were women. Through the stories they shared about feeling sensitive to those identities; however, it was clear that they were collectively embodying more than one of those identity aspects simultaneously. Their strongest expressions of self were the combination of race × gender × academic identities. At college and other social spaces, they were Black, women, and their smart or achiever identity too. They discussed their other identifiers with secondary importance.

Race × Gender × Academic Identity

As Black women high-achievers, they felt pressured to be more successful than others who shared some of their identities. Compared to their peers from home, they shared how their attendance at college meant they had beaten the odds. They were doing better than people they grew up with who were unable to make it out of their environment. "Well, I defied all odds," said Keshia, who described herself as a smart, high-achieving Black woman. She held up her fingers and counted off family and friends who did not make it. "It was just a thing. Like *they* were fighting, *they* were in jail, *they* were into drugs, [and] *they* went to prison. And so to finally be here and have my family behind me supporting me, super proud they can say, 'Yeah, my daughter is at Atlantic. She's a nursing student.' It just makes me feel great." Being successful as a Black woman undergraduate was a big part of how Keshia and several of the students defined themselves.

Michelle felt similarly about her identities, describing herself as a high-achieving and academically talented Black woman. "If I am going to be a Black girl in college, I want to be one of the best Black girls in college," she said. She was particularly aware of what was at stake because she learned about dropout statistics as part of a peer mentoring class. "I don't want to be one of those statistics, even though it's fine if you are: things happen. But I feel like I have to work hard to battle the things that are against me, kind of. Like the numbers are literally against me for being here." Michelle did not want to be one of the capable Black women who did not make it. Her concern about "making it" filled our discussions about how she saw herself and how she thought others did as well.

For Mia, the association between success and her identities was influenced by her family's expectations for her. Her mother often mentioned not getting to go to college herself as an immigrant, but that her expectation was for Mia and her sisters to go to college, provide for themselves, and live comfortably. "I've just always grown up thinking that I would go to college and I would finish college, and then I'd get a job, and maybe I'd like go back to college, but that's always been my main goal." There was as added layer of pressure due to her cousins' poor performance when they attempted college. Several cousins went to college and stopped out because they had babies or did not go back for other reasons. Mia's parents expected her to be the example and to achieve more. "They always say to not make the same mistakes that they've made, to always be better and do the best and keep going." This mix of pressure and support was ingrained in Mia's sense of her intersecting identities. Aisha and Serena's families made them feel pressured as well. As the daughters of immigrants, they all discussed their parents' expectations that they need to be successful and to make the most of opportunities in America that others did not have. For their

West African families, excellence in school and beyond was paramount.

Nicole, who was also West African, felt less pressure once she became a college student but sensed the stigma in her community around professional achievements. Her family called her smart for being good with numbers and took great pride in her accomplishments when she earned high-profile internships and found mentors at big companies. "It's their favorite bragging point," she said. "And like my mom and dad are really supportive, although my dad wanted me to be like a doctor. I think that's kind of like the immigrant African stigma, like you're supposed to be a doctor." While she was in high school he tried to convince her to study medicine despite her interest in finance. Her family stressed the importance of being a young woman who could support herself; at college she demonstrated she was committed to doing so but in a different field than they preferred.

Anissa's family was very pleased with her aspirations to become a doctor. They affirmed her interest in obtaining the pinnacle of their hopes for her status and educational attainment. She said that she just always wanted to be a doctor since she was very young, not because they pushed her to become one, but given how close she was her family, her commitment to that choice was likely influenced by their preferences.

DEFYING STEREOTYPES

Beyond the pressure from their families to excel at a certain level as high-achieving Black women, students also felt pressure to counter a number of stereotypes about achievement for Black women. Those stereotype threats came from the media, interactions with other people and systems at their college, and their prior socialization experiences before attending the university.

The threat of affirming permeating negative images of their identities was ever present in everyday life. Jacqueline described her sensitivity around that issue. " I don't have to subscribe to this dumb race stereotype that has been brought up somewhere along the way. I like reading: I'm going to read. I'm not good at basketball: so what. And it's hard, because that's not a mentality that I think is really prevalent in the Black community." She was committed to doing better than others expected of her. Jacqueline embraced her intelligence as a Black woman in defiance of the stereotype that people like her were unintelligent.

Michelle also felt compelled to do and be better than people expected of her by being a role model for local children of color. She felt particularly aware of her race × gender × academic identity with her "community of successful Black kids" as part of her Black service organization. "We're volunteering at a charter school, and then before we did [a community] center and everything. And that's just really trying to get into the local kids that are predominantly Black and raising them up and showing examples and stuff. So I think, well in [the Black service group], all of them are really important when I'm trying to inspire or empower other people or children. I want to be a Black female college student that's all of these things where people would be looking at me." Creating opportunities for Black children to see real Black college students doing good work was important to Michelle and her peers. She poured into the youth in her community in a way that made her feel good about embodying her identities. Being successful extended to life beyond the classroom for her, and Nicole felt similarly about her own campus involvement.

High achievement extended to Nicole's leadership role as a junior as a co-president of one of her groups. Nicole sensed pressure to be both an outstanding student and leader, sensing her peers' expectation for her to take the lead. "So yeah, just with organization involvement, it makes me just wanna do better for the world, that I don't ever wanna just, I don't want people to be like, 'Oh Nicole, you've really been slacking in helping on this.' And 'Oh no, Nicole like helped me do this. Nicole was an integral part of this initiative' and things like that. So I guess, I guess that makes me wanna be more involved in a way." Nicole felt social pressure from peers to be excellent if she was going to be involved. She needed to achieve inside and outside the classroom to maintain a good impression from others and feel successful.

An observation I noted across the group of students was that they selected their involvement in accord with their identities. For Nicole and Michelle, their organizational involvement was a positive reflection of their most salient identities. Their concern about being more than what others expected of them was iterative of the social norms policing Black women's identity performance. Their performance of self was in constant resistance to the social expectation that they were not supposed to be Black and smart inside or outside the classroom. But this group of Black women persevered under pressure. They illustrated that there were many ways to be a smart Black woman in society, and especially in college. Even in cases where their families were previously unsuccessful at completing college, these women were expected to find a way to make the most of their college opportunity. They were expected to be superwomen high-achievers, and there was no room for error.

RACIALIZED GENDER IDENTITY

Another common stereotype that posed an identity threat for the students was the angry Black woman persona, the infamous cultural construction associated with their race × gender identities. The angry Black woman idea came from media portrayals, wrought with depictions of Black women as aggressive, irrationally upset, and unfeminine. The idea restricted their emotional expressions and labeled them all negative. Instead of acknowledging the systemic and interpersonal issues that confront people like the students in this study, society viewed their expressions of anger, however rational, as unjustified and inappropriate. Knowing that appearing angry would risk reinforcing that behavior, some students held their tongue in class when they disagreed with others.

Shantel reflected on how the concerns she shared about her college experience might be perceived by others. She was self-conscious about expressing herself while not being perceived the way she intended. "If I'm the only Black girl in the class I take notice of that, because it's like, wow. You know, why am I the only Black girl in this classroom? How do I avoid being labeled an angry Black girl? How do I avoid making people uncomfortable, but then why should I?" Shantel was concerned about what people would say if she brought up race or gender in class: two issues that were salient to her diversity course discussion as well as her lived reality. "I just don't want to come across as something that I'm not, you know?" Most striking about Shantel's concern was that she presented an affect as anything but loud or aggressive: in her interviews she spoke softly and avoided eye contact. She even admitted trying her best to avoid people in general. Yet she still felt subject to that assumption about performing Blackness as a Black woman.

Lauryn, who was much more vivacious and opinionated than Shantel, felt the pressure of the same stereotype. She mentioned choosing not to speak up when she disagreed in class. There was tension between wanting to speak up about social issues that matter to her and being labeled an angry Black woman at times when Lauryn was not even angry. "And I think it's really, even in humanities, sometimes we talk about race or something like that. And for some reason, well in the book that we're reading—a lot of them are really old, so they're not so fair to women. So then I think I notice that. But if you always speak up about it, then people will just think you're an angry Black girl. So I think it's definitely hard to, you know? Of course you still want to speak up, so you allow people to think that that's what you are, but it's definitely not there because, you know, that doesn't mean you're angry. It's just you just don't agree."

Being measured in her participation meant that Lauryn had to allow herself to be defined by others' assumptions out of concern for the reaction she might garner if she spoke up.

After reflecting on her college experience, Miranda did describe herself as angry sometimes. After all, she was human. Particularly in light of the glaring social inequities broadcast by the media in the United States at the time, she felt limited in how she could express herself. "At first, I would get angry, and it was a very stifled anger I guess, just because I knew I couldn't actually, like, vocalize my anger because if I vocalize my anger, then I just feed into whatever kind of stereotype they are projecting onto me. If I'm in the classroom and I'm silent for no apparent reason, I just bite my tongue, and I work my way back into conversation in time. I don't interrupt anyone. I try my best not to get into the whole respectability politics things and like, play down parts of my identity, but I also, I don't feel like fighting all the time."

The deaths of Walter Scott and Freddie Gray were still drawing attention in the news and social media during the time of our interviews. All three women had something to say. They did not reference those cases directly but alluded to the issues in the news and media that were on their mind and causing tensions in their communities. They all felt that sharing their perspective would be misunderstood, especially if they displayed any emotion around it. They feared that speaking up, particularly on topics of race or social justice, might allow them to be misperceived. Even when they *were* upset about something that held significance to them, they actively avoided coming off as aggressive, loud, or angry. Those concerns were justified as long as those well-known stereotypes persisted.

Academic Identities

Bright. Talented. Smart. Successful college students had many familiar labels, including the Black women in this study whose family and universities identified them as such. But what did those terms mean to this group of students? They were racial minorities at their PWIs and especially in their honors colleges; did those terms fit their self-perception? Some of the additional honors terms we discussed were high-achieving, smart, and gifted. We also discussed the term academically talented, a concept I thought students may find more inclusive than the other terms based on my work with students of color in my own honors community. These terms were used to understand the students' academic identity.

HIGH-ACHIEVING

Participants described being high-achieving as being a "go-getter," "driven," "disciplined," "getting high grades," and "not willing to settle." Keshia felt the term fit her well. "I see myself as high-achieving because I know that I don't like to settle. I cried when I got a 3.67 GPA this past semester." Standard academic measures of achievement factored into the participants' definitions and performance of being high-achievers. Also common was the idea that high-achievers were willing to put in the work to achieve their goals. Shannon described them as people who "go above and beyond even though they don't have to. So they'll put in extra work to attain their goal . . . they're not just trying to get that easy A." Effort played a role in achieving their goals.

Zoe described herself as a high-achiever, one of those "people who are just always striving to get to a better place than where they are now." Nicole also described herself with this term, noting that high achievement could be inside and outside the classroom. It meant "you're just shooting to do your best and to be the best out of your peers and be at a next level versus everyone else." Amber described herself the same way. And Mia agreed, noting that high-achievers were "always doing a lot, signing up for things, giving back to other people, [and] maybe receiving awards." In contrast to how the literature described the term in reference to honors students, the participants felt high achievement meant more than just SAT scores and GPA. It also did not require natural smarts. "You just try really hard," Lauryn observed. Particularly when they described their own achievements, effort and a sense of agency played a role in whether the participants were successful with their big goals.

The high-achieving label did not fit for a few of the participants because they reasoned that it required giving 100 percent of their effort or attention to something. If they sensed they could give more to some aspect of their involvement or academics, then they would not achieve as highly as they felt capable. Miranda and Crystal were particularly critical of their achievements. As Crystal explained, "I walk away from opportunities a lot, just because I feel like I have too many, and I don't want to overwhelm myself. So sometimes I'll just opt out of applying for something or, you know, signing up for the extra seminar or something. Because I know that I want to go, and I know I'm interested in this, but I do not have the time, and I can't give it 100 percent." As a very involved student leader who was also focused on her academics, limitations on her time prevented her from achieving all the things she could. Crystal was less involved in campus life than she perceived her peers were and agreed that her lack of effort kept her from achieving, but she believed she would be a better, higher-achiever if she actually applied herself. Being high-achieving would mean "accomplishing all the things that I've set out for myself . . . maybe even accomplishing things that I never perceived . . . I was able to." Crystal's assessment of her college performance was that she had yet to reach that level but she had the potential.

SMART

Being smart was one of the most common terms associated with honors students. Most of the students felt they were smart, although some acknowledged the term more willingly than others. Participants defined smart as "intelligent," "book smart," and "academic success." Keshia defined the term by saying, "It just means that they do well in academics. I think when people look at honor students and say we're smart, they're like, 'Oh, you get your A's in your classes, you know a lot of things, you do well in college classes.'" As Keshia's description suggested, for many of the students being smart was associated with good grades and performing well on tests.

Students in the study also expected that smart meant particular characteristics and behaviors that test scores did not measure. Smart could be performative. Grace was talented in the arts: she sang and played multiple instruments. "I think it ties in with being good at things. Being good at playing an instrument would mean that you're smart musically," Grace shared. "Or if you're good at coming up with ideas, then you're smart intellectually." Zoe felt that being smart means "knowing yourself, plus a willingness to learn or an eagerness to learn, and then the ability to use the information that you have resourceful[ly]." Aisha and Jacqueline agreed. "I feel like smart is someone who knows a lot of things, who knows how to apply the knowledge that they know," Aisha shared. Jacqueline noted that "it's not enough to just know the facts from the textbook. You have to be able to make them actionable and put them into context." It was important to continue gaining knowledge and understand how to apply it.

There was a difference between book smarts and street smarts, and many noted that the kind associated with honors students tended not to be street smarts. They supposed that a person who was smart should also have common sense, but this was a quality "which a lot of people lack," according to Amber. "I have engineering friends who are brilliant, absolutely brilliant, but can't function sometimes." Serena and Jacqueline echoed Amber's sentiments. Mia felt that an important part of being smart was "knowing what's right and what's wrong" and making good decisions. "I try not to base intelligence off of test scores or anything. It's more about the person and how they react to things." Simply being book smart and able to do well in classes did not mean that a person was smart in every area of her life.

Perceptions about the amount of agency required to be labeled or perform smartness varied among academically talented Black women: it could be innate or a product of effort. Lauryn described both in her definition of smart and felt the term did not apply to her. "Well, I guess that there's some people who are naturally 'smart,' and they may be very good at math or science or something like that. But then I think there's also people who just work really hard to do better, and so they would be considered smart too. I mean, I think it's a hard word because sometimes people will be like, 'Oh, you're so smart,' but really if they just worked the same amount, then they would really be in the same place. So sometimes, it's kind of like that." Lauryn felt that other people could improve their grades or academic performance by working hard like people who are labeled smart. Anissa felt the same way, particularly as applied to one of her friends from high school whom she considered smart but was lazy. "Anyone can be smart if they try. It's not something you're born with." Anissa's view was evident in how she described encouraging her high school friend to go to class and do his homework so he would get better grades. According to Nicole, students would be "taking that extra mile to study versus just getting by" if they were smart. There was agency in determining if a student would be considered smart, based on Lauryn, Anissa, and Nicole's ideas. Studying, being diligent, and working hard could pay off.

Although most participants felt that it was a compliment to be described as smart, a few acknowledged that there could be a stigma associated with the term, particularly as they reflect on how they were treated in other contexts. "I used to think it was an insult back in the day. Like 'Oh, you're so *smart*.' The way people would say it. It's like oh, is that not a good thing to be smart? [But] doesn't that take you places?" Nicole's peers tried to make her feel bad about having good academic performance, insinuating that it was different in a bad way and not okay to be smart.

Miranda had another definition of smart. "Even when I was younger, actually, it was kind of used to punish me a little bit. It's like, 'Are you trying to be smart?' Like you had an attitude." In familial context, when she needed to be respectful of authority, it could be inappropriate to be smart or behave like a know-it-all. Other students shared similar school-age experiences as well and alluded to the role those earlier experiences played in how well the list of honors identities described them. The variety of connotations for this term suggested that the participants received mixed messages from their social, academic, and familial environments about the meaning of their smart identity and whether it was something constructive or socially acceptable.

ACADEMICALLY TALENTED

I introduced the term academically talented to add more inclusive language to the discourse on honors students. Participants described the academically talented as people who "perform better in classes," are "good at schoolwork," and are "book smart." Amber described being academically talented as related to the "the amount that you put into learning that material. I think you can be talented, but not get the results that you want, because you don't put the work into it." Putting in work was also key to Anissa's understanding of the term. "You have to study to be academically talented. You can't just, you know, just read the book and then go take a test. That isn't going to get you a good grade on the test. You're not understanding the material you're just knowing it. I feel like if you don't apply it, I don't think you're academically talented in my opinion." Application and effort mattered in many of the other participants' definitions as well. In contrast, Crystal felt the term referred to an innate quality. "I think talent's also something that you're naturally good at, so it's just where you thrive, and academics is for academically talented." Participants had a lot of opinions about the term but included the term in their self-description.

Michelle felt the term fit her. She described academically talented people as "good at schoolwork. So, good at studying and organizing, getting things in on time, and asking questions. Just good at figuring out how they can learn stuff." Serena adopted the term as well, suggesting it referred to excelling at school, understanding concepts, and passing tests. Nicole liked calling herself academically talented as well. It meant "you get really good grades. Maybe you know how to finesse a test and can really make a good, write a good paper and sound eloquent. I think that just means you're a superstar in school, in your classes and stuff like that. Academically talented, yeah, a smarty pants basically, but not in a sassy way." As Nicole's definition suggested, ascriptions of ability could be associated with having an attitude or an air of arrogance. She was careful to clarify her meaning.

A number of the definitions associated academically talented with the other honors labels, particularly among students who indicated it was not a salient part of their identity. Shantel indicated that she felt "like that's another word for smart, academically talented. They're good at school or good at school-related things." Amber related the term with the idea of smart as well. And Shannon felt the terms were similar too, but academically talented had a different tone than smart, though she could not describe the differences she sensed. "I feel like a student would be someone who, like I want to say someone who's actually really interested in what they're learning. They're not just trying to get the grade, but they really are taking it. They want to do something with that work, but also it somehow comes easy to them, the talent aspect. Because I feel like a talent is something that comes naturally, we don't have to work at it." Shannon went on to indicate that academically talented was the same as smart, and gifted and academically talented were the same.

GIFTED

Many of the student constructions of the term gifted were associated with innate abilities or biology, and only one participant described herself as gifted. Nicole described a gifted person as "someone that's just a little bit smarter or does better in the subject or something like that. They're wired differently so that they're, they can go to the next level in that subject." Others said gifted people had "special talents," were "born smart," or had a "natural" ability to do well at something on the first try. People could be gifted academically or in music, art, sports, or other extracurricular endeavors.

A few of the students associated the term with their participation in special programs in primary or secondary school: they took achievement or IQ tests and were placed into resource or project classes to enhance their academic curriculum. At this point in their academic careers, however, they no longer felt that label was appropriate for them. Crystal reflected on being gifted as a child and the differences she feels in her aptitude as a college student. "I used to think I was, I guess gifted, but that has since changed since entering college. So, just, I was definitely the person in high school that didn't try. I could listen and, you know, I guess internalize and regurgitate later, 'cause that's all learning is in high school. And now that it's not internalize and regurgitate, it's more like internalize and apply, it's not, I can't excel the way I used to or excel in the same manner." In college, the expectations for learning and understanding information were different than in high school: Crystal felt she was not gifted anymore because she could not use the same effortless approach to learning from prior educational environments. She described a common transition issue many new college students faced: formerly successful learning or memorization methods in their high school classroom were not a good fit for the demands of their rigorous collegiate environment. The new teaching and learning environment required the need to adapt their learning style.

Anissa's definition was consistent with other participants but drew attention to other factors in the outcomes associated with giftedness. "I feel like when people use the word gifted it seems inherent. Like the child was born with it. But I feel like you're not born intelligent or academically talented, it's something you achieve over time. It's based on your circumstance and how you're brought up and what your own personal goals are and based on what your parents instill in you." Jacqueline described herself as gifted and agreed with Anissa's assessment. There was more than biology involved in being good at things: there were sociocultural and economic privileges that catalyzed those abilities.

The underlying tone of the students' discussions about their academic identities implied that students were socialized not to talk about how intelligent or accomplished they were, especially as Black women. There was palpable tension between being their honors identities and feeling comfortable acknowledging those abilities. Michelle's perceptions illustrated that concern. "I feel like, oh, I'm showing off if I say I'm smart and academically talented. But I feel like I wouldn't be here if I wasn't." She was reluctant to own her academic identifiers because she felt it was "show offy." She explained why she felt that way about being smart: "Because self-praise is kind of like, I don't know . . . It's not as if it's looked down on, but you kind of look at people sideways when they talk about how great they are, even though everyone's supposed to be proud of all of their things that they've achieved and how good they are at things. But then when you talk about it, it's like, stop." Michelle alluded to the mixed messages she received about having pride in her achievements.

Instead of touting their own accomplishments, Keshia and Shantel mentioned that others would describe them as high-achieving. Though Shantel did not like the labels for herself, her family would feel differently. "So I know that my mom would use the word 'smart' to describe me, academically talented, high-achieving because whenever I get, like all my report cards, if they were good, which they usually were—like straight As and stuff like that—she would put it on Facebook, show all her friends, tell everybody, you know. So I know that she's proud of me as far as that goes, and she would describe me as smart." It was all right for others, but not for these students, to acknowledge their abilities. And because of their prior academic achievement, family often assumed they would get good grades and did not ask about their other needs or issues that could impact their success.

Identities and Academics

Study participants critiqued their major curricula and other required courses for the glaring absence of the experiences of people of color in their syllabi. In the limited instances when a variety of racial, gender, or other identity groups were mentioned in the class topics, they addressed surface level ideas. Students perceived those topics as curricular after-thoughts. The lack of writers and textbooks about or by their own racial and other backgrounds was noticeable.

Mia noticed this issue in her courses. "The content we cover in class, I feel like it's very exclusive of certain groups. And some professors will attempt to be inclusive, but it's very preliminary," Mia observed. "They don't really go in depth, they just touch on something." As a political science major, Miranda's program exposed her to broad ideas such as how different populations tend to vote, but beyond the demographic statistics, there was no discussion of why, based on those people's various identities or life experiences. Over three years of classes, the texts in her major coursework did not reflect any aspects of her own background or her community's experiences. Miranda mentioned that, in one of her classes, "we read one Toni Morrison book, and every other book was by a White male author, centered White male protagonists, and it was draining. So as much as I like some of my classes, I still have classes where that's the norm and no one notices." This token representation sent the message that the experiences of people like Miranda were not important to discuss in academic spaces or her professional field.

As a social science major, Shantel was particularly cognizant of the absence of writers from her own background across her academic coursework. In her required humanities course, she knew the professor's objective was to challenge students' perspectives of the world, but she had her own ideas on how to do so. "Then I can think of quite a few that would . . . I would hope would open the eyes of some people because we have issues on the home front. And if he's trying to get us to see things from a different perspective, then I think there should definitely be some literature from authors of color who are talking about their experiences as a person of color here in America. That's a really important perspective to try to understand. Um . . . and it's useful because you . . . I dunno. It's not to say that you won't take anything away from the *Epic of Gilgamesh*, but . . . I didn't . . ." Excluding the voices of people of color from the curriculum was a historical systemic issue; in an increasingly diverse society and with more diverse students in college classrooms, universities need to remedy that limitation of the curricula across academic majors.

BEING THE ONLY ONE

A common experience among the students was perceiving they were the only one with their identities in their classrooms. Especially in their honors courses, they were "painfully aware," as Anissa put it, that they were different. Their minority status in class—as the only Black student or the only woman in science or math—meant their performance of their visible identities carried the weight of representation and tokenization. In the absence of other people of color, students described how their behaviors could be attributed to their Blackness and womanhood instead of the student identity they had in common with classmates.

Being the "only one" was especially imposing in class on the topic of race. Often the only Black woman in her courses, Mia was frustrated about the way discussions of race made it hard to be in the classroom. "I don't feel like I have to speak on behalf of the entire Black community, but people always expect me to," she said. Being the spokesperson for her race or other identities was not a role Mia desired. Nor did Jacqueline, but she often felt compelled to "enlighten" her classmates.

The readings for the required diversity course Jacqueline was enrolled in introduced students to a different marginalized group each week, and the focus on breadth limited the depth of study of various racial groups. Because the texts were not a complete reflection of the lived experiences of the populations they studied, Jacqueline's peers would ask her about her own experiences as an African American. She admitted feeling uneasy in the days leading up to the readings on her racial group. "I felt like I was inherently dreading having to go into class that Friday because I knew this would be the week I'd have to speak the most." She felt that way because other classroom experiences had conditioned her to anticipate the need to be spokesperson, though she had some reluctance to serve in that role. "I know that's kind of a selfish thing to say, but I'm not here to educate anybody, you know. I'm trying to do my own thing. And so if some of the texts that we chose could in themselves give a more complete picture, people wouldn't feel like they had to come to me to fill in the gaps." Jacqueline felt compelled to represent her identity groups, despite her apparent discomfort, because her peers would not get insight from their texts. Miranda also problematized being the educator on race in her classroom: "It's not my job to educate someone else about [race], so sometimes not talking about it is okay, because I would rather have good discussions that actually help everyone involved than have discussions where I constantly feel like I have to explain things or answer for my whole race or just things like that. I'd rather just not." For both students, the classroom presented a burden to educate others about her background as if it were representative of what all African Americans experience.

Shannon alluded to this concern about representing as well, particularly as it related to how she was perceived in the classroom. "In a school setting, I just try to be that high-achieving student. I don't feel like I'm representing all Trinidadian women in the world or Black women. I'm just trying to be myself, but I know that my actions or whatever could set a path for someone else to have a good impression on someone." Shannon understood that her achievements and performance might impact future students who look like her and so she behaves in a way that curried favor. "That's not my goal: I'm just trying to be the best version of myself," she added. In her description of her intentions, Shannon rejects the burden of being a model student to debunk assumptions instructors might make about her racial or other visible identities. This imbalance between her own desires for the version of herself she wanted to present versus the performance she put on for others meant she was constantly monitoring herself, thinking about the weight of her actions and how they would impact her image (and others like her). Shannon's self-description fit the pattern of the burden of representation that many of the other students acknowledged influenced their classroom behavior.

Secondary Identities

For people living at the intersections of multiple oppressions, it could be difficult to filter which identities matter more than others. As part of their participation in the study, the women had an opportunity to reflect on the relative importance of their multifaceted selves. Grounded in the focus of the study, students led their discussion of what it meant to be their authentic selves with their racial, ethnic, gender, student, and academic selves. Students created their own list of self-identifiers during the first interview and had the opportunity to reflect on and revise them in the second interview. Across the cohort of women in the study, there were several aspects of who they were that they chose not to discuss without my asking. Their spiritual, political, and sexual orientation identifiers were among the commonly omitted ones from their first interview and were generally excluded from their lists for a second time in the next interview. When asked about them, students had a variety of reactions. Some participants expressed that they chose not to share those identities on their list because they were private. Most were willing to classify themselves into membership in associated groups when I asked in the second interview. I analyzed the relative importance of the identities that many of the women described as playing little to no role in how they made meaning of their experiences at college. As I imagined the possibility for interventions that could make campus and their college experience more nurturing, the omission meant as much to understanding how they made meaning about their experiences and environment as the ones they selected.

SPIRITUALITY

Only three students brought up their spirituality during their first interviews. And after further discussion in the second interviews, most students still did not include their spiritual identity in their lists. Mia identified herself as having grown up Catholic but rarely went to mass during the semester. Before the start of our second meeting, Anissa mentioned attending church fairly regularly but did not offer spirituality as a part of her self-descriptors. Serena also left Christianity off of her list. She felt her other identities were more important. Michelle's family was Christian on one parent's side and Muslim on the other, and her parents intentionally observed neither in her household. Similarly, Lauryn mentioned being active in her church community at home but felt that the conflict between her spiritual identity and sexual orientation made that complicated. "If I go to anything that's church related, you notice that you're gay. But nobody . . . they might not notice it, but you think about it," Lauryn reflected. Spirituality did not hold a place at the core of most of the women's self-concept.

Zoe had a mostly Muslim family but did not identify as Muslim herself. The aunt she was closest with associated herself with Oshun and Yoruba African spiritual practices. She did not feel any of those were important parts of who she was or how she saw the world. Jacqueline's parents were Southern Baptist and Catholic and exposed her to both kinds of church as a child but felt that her own definition was unclear. Shannon's family identified as Christian when they were in the Caribbean, but not since living in America. Some of the students left their spirituality off of their list because it was more associated with their families than with their own identity.

SOCIAL CLASS

Students were aware of varying economic backgrounds among their friends and peers but sensed that at their urban university it was not a major point of concern when interacting with other students. Some of the students offered vivid descriptions of their observations of social class markers where they grew up. They noticed peers with expensive cars or bags or who lived on the nicer side of town. They were less sensitive to, or acknowledged fewer of those markers, in their college lives. As Miranda observed, living in a city, most people took public transportation to get places, so it was hard to see the indicators of social status the way she could in high school. But since Miranda worked to pay her own bills, she alluded to her awareness of some peers needing jobs in college and others who had more privileged financial circumstances. Crystal and Keshia lived with other women whose families paid for all of their college expenses, including giving them spending money. Their own families did not do that for them: in one case because they did not have the means and the other did not want them to because she preferred to be independent. The disparity in financial status among the roommates was very noticeable but not so much among their classmates.

A few acknowledged that Atlantic University was in a predominantly low-income neighborhood, which seemed to draw some stigma from peers. The university had a legacy for providing educational opportunities for working-class people. This was reflected in its diverse undergraduate population, which included a number of nontraditional and part-time students, often from the local area. Jacqueline was frustrated by her peers who conflated race with poverty. "Another stereotype of Black culture, aside from being like well you're Black so you're dumb, is you're Black so you're poor." One edge of Atlantic University was bordered by a low-income housing community, which seemed to impact how people perceived her on campus, assuming she was a local resident. "And so it's hard having two identities that don't, in most people's minds, coexist together, you know. Being an upper-middle-class African American person or just being an upper-middle-class person in general around here." The assumed intersections of race and class make Jacqueline feel uncomfortable. Why was it so hard for her classmates to believe a person of color could choose to attend

Atlantic without being from the (low-income) neighborhood? And why such negativity about the possibility she could be a local?

Polytech University was a private, more selective institution located in a business district but had a less wealthy neighborhood not too far away. Polytech's higher tuition meant more economically privileged students. Shannon could definitely see signs of people's affluence there. "I'm pretty aware of it. I think based off of all of my friends—all of my friends have part time jobs and we are all like, 'Let's not go out tonight, we can't spend the money.' But it is Polytech, so our students do have more money and probably don't have a job, and their parents pay for everything. And then just being in this city you see poverty." Her family helped her out with tuition, but Shannon also identified herself as someone who knew she needed to be employed to have access to what she needed for college. She proudly worked and had several highly paid internships to be able to afford her lifestyle.

POLITICAL STANCE

The political science majors were the only participants who felt their political identities mattered in their self-descriptions. "I think in college it's kind of one of those things that's assumed, especially in an urban setting, that everyone's liberal. I don't necessarily think that's the case," Miranda observed. She thought her peers were not critical about politics and noticed from her interactions with peers that they felt it was "just whatever. It doesn't really matter," when she felt passionately that there were issues that affected her life and other students collectively.

Serena mentioned that she was a liberal but did not really talk about it much in our discussions. Others omitted their political identity as a self-identifier out of concern for being judged based on those identities, particularly within the context of the charged political climate at the time. Data collection for the study coincided with the spring before a contentious 2016 presidential election in the United States. Atlantic University had a reputation as predominantly liberal and accepting, but some of the students admitted that they were avoiding voicing their alliances and opinions about politics, and other group membership, in most contexts—especially socially and on social media—because they were trying to avoid backlash from peers. Zoe felt that accepting a political label might be used to assume other things about who she was or what she believed, but she also felt she was more than that one identity. "My decision to vote does not solely depend on my age and my so called entitlement. It also depends on my race and my gender, because we are all intersectional beings. We are not just one thing. Not a single one of us. We're not Black in one moment or White in one moment and then transgender in another moment and then female—that's not how it works. So who I vote for is not just because I'm a millennial and I want free education. It's also because like I'm Black and I want someone to think about the human rights that Black people deserve that they aren't getting or like all of these other things." The presidential election season made Zoe and other participants feel particularly sensitive about the significance of that aspect of her identity. And given the racially and politically charged nature of the discourse around the election, safety was a good reason to keep those group memberships private as well.

SEXUAL ORIENTATION

Another potentially sensitive identity was students' sexual orientation. Most of the participants indicated that they were straight, but as people who identified themselves with heterosexual social norms, that made sexual orientation less salient for Shannon, Zoe, and Miranda. Each noted that she did not pay attention to that aspect of her identity. Zoe described herself as "normal," Shannon mentioned her boyfriend, and Miranda said she was cisgender and straight. Initially, they did not mention it as part of how they identified. Choosing not to notice this aspect of who they were could mean it mattered more to their sense of self than they wanted to admit. It could also mean they lived in a context where it was unimportant at the time. Despite their claims, it was possible and likely that they could identify otherwise but did not want to out themselves.

A few other women addressed the heteronormativity that limited their sexual expression. They were very astutely aware of their differences from mainstream society, particularly as they were in the midst of their identity development in that aspect of their lives. The Black queer, bisexual, and lesbian women were aware of how the intersections could complicate their participation in social spaces designed to support only one of those identities. Michelle noted that it was hard to be Black and queer on campus because she had difficulty finding other Black people who shared this identity. Lauryn noticed the racial gap in the lesbian, gay, bisexual, and transgender (LGBT) community, too. To be queer was to be perceived as minority among the minorities.

As a peer mentor in the sexuality center on campus, Lauryn was critical of the lack of people of color on the staff. "I feel like a lot of the people who are in the center are really aware of LGBT stuff, but they're almost all White in there. Which I think is, you notice a difference." Lauryn perceived there was a visible lack of intersectional support on issues of race and gender identity at her university. In campus life, Serena noticed that she was usually in a group that only addressed one of her identities at a time, not all of them. She also felt that being at college made it easier for her to embrace her sexual orientation: "I was able to think about more, being bisexual because I did it. Most of the, 'cause it was really tough you know. Back in, when I was in high school, you didn't really see, or everyone was either gay or straight or a lesbian, and then you still didn't really see the LGBT or you didn't see those other groups that were not heterosexual. So I didn't really, I kinda, I think I put that in the back of my mind and because of that I didn't really, I just didn't address that part, the other side of me." Once Serena got to college, she felt she was allowed space and time to develop psychosocially in a way that she felt inhibited in high school. Her reflection on her sexual orientation demonstrated an awareness of the sociopolitical challenges of being a Black woman among the other identities and the ways society viewed people like her. The concerns of the queer Black women in the study underpinned the need for existing campus organizations to be more inclusive of people like them who live at the intersections of sometimes competing social identity groups.

Analysis of Identities

An understanding of how this group of talented Black women undergraduates made meaning around their identities assumes their perceptions of their college experience were influenced by their social position at the intersection of several discriminated groups. The way students described their identities reflected the way they were socialized, the internalization of mainstream social norms, and expectations from peers and family in their precollege and collegiate interactions. Students' descriptions of their interactions in interpersonal, organizational, and other social spaces illustrated the relative importance and intersections of their identities. Although the students had common social group membership, they were not monolithic: their unique backgrounds and perspectives meant they showed up differently and had varied perceptions of their identities, including their hesitance to or intersectional affirmation of the salience of their various identities (Porter et al., 2020).

Despite fitting their own definitions of smart, high-achieving, academically talented, or gifted, many of the students were reluctant to adopt the academic identity terms. They alluded to the problematic ways their peers or others might perceive them if they acknowledged their achievements and abilities. There was tension between the ways they could describe people just like them and what it would signify to others if they referred to themselves that way.

Students expressed concern about how they would be perceived by their peers and society more broadly if they brought attention to their achievements by accepting the high-achieving label. They received mixed messages about how acceptable that would be. There was the risk of seeming arrogant, elitist, or overly confident: all were offensive to peers and family. They had to behave modestly to avoid negative labels. Despite the various constructive and judgmental connotations it carried, most participants were willing to own that term as part of their identity. Honors communities, especially those created by and for students of color, held the potential to offer more nurturing spaces that enable fuller self-expression of that aspect of who talented Black women truly were.

Numerous participants stressed the importance of natural talent or giving full effort to their goals as part of the reason for their achievement. Although those ideas played a role in their performance, they were all intrinsic explanations of success. They ignored the systemic barriers that often limited the access to resources or social capital that could enhance their ability to succeed. For example, access to test and study prep, academic coaching, tutoring, or exposure to advanced coursework varied among college students, all of which prepared students for college success. The challenges inside and outside the classroom drew attention to those barriers. Neglecting external influences on their performance meant students may blame themselves for not achieving to their full potential, when in reality it was a combination of internal and less visible external obstacles. Their perceived and tangible barriers got in the way of them being even more accomplished than they were at the time of the study.

Despite mentioning how some of the achievement terms did not fit, participants' definitions were fairly descriptive of their own academic outcomes and performance. The disconnection with the terms implied a social stigma that people in this population were not commonly associated with intelligence. It also signaled the need for a revision in the language used to describe honors students—methodologically as well as in practice—to enhance how faculty and staff supported and recruited talented Black women. As the sample for this qualitative study was not representative of the greater population of all Black undergraduate women in honors colleges, more research on academic identity terms and adding the term academically talented to the discourse still had potential benefit for future research.

Students described their status as the only one in their classrooms as inducing pressure to perform in a particular way, isolating, and as attracting unwanted attention from their peers and instructor. Being the only one as an identity experience in this study was consistent with findings in prior studies focused on Black women, undergraduates, and of Black high-achievers (Patton, Evans-Winters, & Jacobs, 2022; Winkle-Wagner, 2009; Fries-Britt, 1998). Despite their intellectual ability to excel in the class, the conditions were unsupportive.

The students' discussions of how they made meaning around the facets of their identities sparked more questions about the experiences of this talented group of students. They described constant pressure because of their identities from peers, their environment, and family. How could a person fit in enough to feel comfortable in an environment where they feel othered but still feel like their authentic self? And how sustainable is that kind of survival? How does the pressure to be excellent manifest and what is the outcome for students like the ones in this study? Is it the drive for overinvolvement like Nicole? Is it internalization that results in stress or irrational self-expectations? Is it ever acceptable to express anger, particularly as a Black woman? Could anger expression become acceptable because of things that happen in daily life, or because of issues in the news that impact people in her community or who look like her? And is it not a natural human reaction to have feelings about those things? When would it be safe and celebrated for the talented Black women living at the intersections of racial, gender, academic, and other systems of power to authentically express themselves at college or beyond? Smart Black women yearned for and deserved an opportunity to be in a collegiate environment that did not police their self-expression and allowed them to be their authentic selves.

~ 6 ~

Implications for Practice

By illuminating the threats and successes of college life for the students in my study, I hope that this book can empower and prepare other talented Black women undergraduates who may also face those negative interactions. Developing supportive campuses that address the unique needs of talented Black women requires intentional efforts from university administration that take intersections of identity into consideration. Intersectionality provided a valuable lens to examine the contexts, interactions, and experiences of the high-achieving undergraduate Black women in the study. At its core, intersectionality argued for the importance of considering people multidimensionally, noting that each person was more than their outward presentation of their perceived race or gender; they were both of those things, as well as the combination of all the mutually influential identities in between. Students in the study acknowledged the threats to their identities and were cognizant of the role those threats played in being ignored or erased or prejudged in their interactions with peers and instructors.

From a structural perspective, intersectionality also provided a framework to craft organizational solutions. Campus life was both a reflection and a microcosm of society. Systemic issues such as racism, sexism, and classism all played a role in the students' college experience. From the lack of racial diversity in their predominantly White honors colleges to the exclusion of diverse voices in their curricula, oppressive forces and social norms were existent in every context. Students' membership in more than one socially oppressed group necessitated that those same identities that factored into their experiences should also play a role in any solutions aiming to support them (Porter et al., 2020; Patton & Croom, 2017; Hancock, 2007; Stewart, 2009). In this way, intersectionality functioned as a critical way to offer alternative practices to address the injustices operating in university spaces. This book provided data that can drive policy changes and programmatic initiatives to foster more inclusive university environments. Creating spaces and environments that affirm talented Black women's multifaceted identities, cultivating campus networks, and improving faculty and staff of color representation were among the key improvements grounded in the findings. All of these recommendations applied to universities broadly but there were also additional considerations for honors communities specifically.

Cultivating Spaces and Communities

The experiences of academically talented Black women in campus life reinforced the need for PWIs to address the tone of the various spaces that high-achieving Black women occupy. How welcome or othered students felt inside and outside the classroom mattered; it played a role in their impressions of the university and their place—or lack thereof—within their social or academic communities. From the residence halls to student organizations, students felt noticeably different from their peers who shared few aspects of their identity, especially racially or academically. Many of the students were bothered by the lack of racial and other kinds of diversity at their PWI; social opportunities to connect with other talented Black students, especially women, would enhance their connection to the university.

Staff need to create or reform existing spaces to serve as hubs for gatherings, where academically talented Black women undergraduates (and other minoritized groups among high-achievers) can privately vent, reflect, and process their experiences navigating their PWI in a supportive environment, without the gaze of their White peers. Without these psychological supports, Black women high-achievers' mental health and well-being are at risk (Jerald et al., 2017; Byrd & Porter, 2022).

Optimally, students would feel empowered to organically have their own gatherings in existing spaces to foster community as well. Especially after major social issues impact their various identity communities, having the resources to gather in solidarity would help students feel at home. A first step in creating those spaces is assessing how supportive places like women's, LGBT, or Black student centers are for high-achieving Black women and taking action on student feedback (as suggested by research on Black women in Patton & Croom, 2017.). If there is not staff support for discussion groups like sista circles or spaces are not accessible, students can be encouraged to tap into virtual ones by following podcasts or joining in virtual community discussions with other talented Black women. Digital connections can reduce feelings of campus isolation, foster retention, and bring groups of talented Black women closer together (Robinson & Williams, 2022). There must be a demonstration of support from the university, including the commitment of human resources and financial support, to sustain advocacy efforts (Steele, 2022). Colleges cannot simply expect that high-achieving Black women will figure it out on their own: there must be a commitment to their success. And staff who advocate for these students need to be willing to listen and to take bold action to make environments more welcoming, even when they are critical of the university.

Part of the challenge of being the only one in the classroom or in student groups was lacking supportive peers to help survive those experiences. Some participants suggested having Black women honors peer mentors help younger peers navigate college, particularly their honors experience. Having an upper-class student who shares several of their identities impart their insider knowledge of their campus, assist with the transition to college, and be a first friend would offer a great deal of support. Peer mentoring was common in a variety of special interest communities at universities, including some honors colleges. Giving students the option to select a peer mentor or mentee who shares some of their identities could make those programs more affirming for talented Black women seeking connections. A student also suggested a welcome event for high-achieving students of color to help connect them with research opportunities, finding balance, learning about university resources, and find potential mentors. Her idea was a modification of an institute for STEM students of color that she attended. Such programs help disrupt narratives about how Black women fit into STEM (Joseph, 2022) and other academic disciplines and do not require much additional resources to produce. Whether formal or informal, research showed that students in constructive mentoring relationships were retained, had a sense of connection with their institution, and were satisfied with their college experience, particularly students of color (Bledsoe & Rome, 2006; Baker, 2006). This was also the case for Black women (Commodore, Baker, & Arroyo, 2018).

A sense of tension between their desire to be good students and their peers' expectations that they would behave in the stereotypical manner was an identity-related issue for the students. To avoid the spotlight, they chose silence. But limited participation from high-achieving Black women in the classroom did not signify a lack of interest. As with their measured contributions to discussions, often the students were very interested in the subject matter, or even mastered it but did not feel empowered to share their insights in class. Faculty must enhance classroom environments by creating opportunities for student discussion without putting students of color in the hot seat to enlighten their peers about race.

Classroom experiences could be enriched by the inclusion of more voices of color in the physical space and the curriculum. And a more diverse set of learners and instructors would help high-achieving Black women feel less othered in the classroom for their racial, economic, nationality, or other identities. Faculty and academic departments should make intentional efforts to enhance curricula by adding authors of historically underrepresented populations to their syllabi and course offerings. Sharing that information on the department website would signal to students that their department was open to and welcomed their unique backgrounds and experiences to the classroom.

Faculty Development

Instructors should be the foundation of inclusion instead of a potential source of the isolation and silencing that students in the study encountered in their classrooms. At colleges like

Atlantic and Polytech Universities, students may stumble upon the occasional professor of color. Envision how empowering it would be for Black women high-achievers to have a professor who shared their identities, especially in an honors program where they were so often the only person of color in their classrooms. As a professional Black woman high-achiever in her own right, this professor's presence could reshape power dynamics about whose knowledge and contributions in the classroom mattered. Similarly, an even greater impact could be affected by a White instructor who was keen on supporting the voices of all of the students in the class, not just the outspoken and confident majority students who occupied a privileged space of authority in classroom discussions.

The students in this book considered faculty and staff of color role models, potential mentors, and allies in stereotype-busting against majority students. Hiring more qualified faculty and staff of color would be paramount for Black women high-achievers but also for students of other races as well, debunking the idea of who gets to be in the position of professor. Regardless of identity, all faculty have the power to make an impact by helping all students develop the analytical tools to constructively discuss issues in class among people with dissenting ideas and with cultural sensitivity. Part of this also entails directly addressing bias-related or insensitive language students may use to talk about or around their peers in class discussions. One strategy suggested by a study participant was to model analyzing and discussing course readings, then gradually allow students to facilitate their own discussions and teachings, with the instructor's guidance. University support to help faculty more confidently manage those discussions is essential and readily available at campus teaching and learning centers.

Another strategy for faculty is to assign texts about or by diverse populations (e.g., race, gender, national origin) and assess students in ways that demonstrate they have a good understanding of the issues. Students suggested guided discussions or analytical book reviews. A successful integration of the content and the evaluation would signal to students that the inclusion of multicultural texts was not a token afterthought.

Enhancing Honors Colleges

As an honors educator and a researcher-practitioner, there were clear applications of the findings for developing honors-specific support strategies. Recruiting and retaining students, faculty, and staff of color; soliciting honors courses on diverse communities; and creating communities within honors were the key recommendations.

Active and intentional recruitment of students of color to join honors would further diversify the academic and social aspects of the honors experience. Students' concern about being the only one and feeling different in the classroom and residence halls would be alleviated by the presence of more underrepresented students in those spaces. Those students would also illustrate the diversity of backgrounds and experiences among students of color to White peers in the program and broaden their perspectives about whom and what an honors student looks like. Study participants suggested targeting recruitment efforts toward high-achieving students at their alma maters and at schools with high populations of students of color. Honors can also recruit undergraduates from among its own university, encouraging minoritized students—particularly those in student organizations—to apply for admission.

This research brought attention to the ways honors colleges needed to do more to consider the needs of the Black women in their programs, echoing earlier calls to action (Freeman, 1999). More faculty and staff of color were needed, and there must be opportunities for community building to enhance the honors experience for high-achieving Black women.

Faculty and staff of color have the power to shift the potentially demeaning honors classrooms and hostile social environments into safe spaces on campus. When they can also serve as vocal advocates, mentors, and role models, professionals of color can help all honors students have a more dynamic learning experience. Connecting high-achieving Black women with supportive scholars and mentors across campus, even non-honors instructors and staff, would give them a better sense of support from their honors participation. The small number of faculty of color in honors at the PWIs in this study was reflective of the systemic barriers in society that manifest on college campuses.

From my professional background in honors education, I had knowledge of the variations in honors admissions practices at institutions. Some only screened students for honors participation as part of the institution's admissions process for incoming first-year students. Precollege indicators, such as test scores, advanced coursework, and GPA, were most important in those cases and were often tied to university merit-based aid. In some of those cases the university admissions office manages honors admission as well. Other universities allow current students or transfer students to apply directly to honors. Consideration for admission is based on college GPA and essays or references; this kind of process was often managed by the honors college itself. More holistic honors review processes would consistently consider students' demonstration of leadership, community engagement, and demonstration of overcoming personal or academic challenges. Common methods of selection for honors often leave this piece out of the admissions process, potentially overlooking a number of qualified candidates. In order to see change, universities have to be willing to address recruitment and hiring processes that may limit access to candidates of color.

Many honors programs solicit departments or instructors to offer honors seminars or specialized sections of their courses for honors students. Honors administrators can tailor those calls for proposals to create an imperative for courses that reflect the diverse backgrounds and interests of students in their programs. Black women do not have the responsibility to educate their honors peers about what it means to be their various identities; instead courses focused on Black feminism, women's rights, historical representation of people of color in the media, or other topics grounded in research or the experiences of marginalized communities can offer students material from which to learn. Faculty whose areas of expertise include underrepresented communities or social justice topics should be recruited to teach in honors and compensated for sharing their knowledge with the honors community beyond the classroom as well. Another approach is to offer pedagogical support for honors instructors that encourages them to reflect on their inclusion of voices of scholars from underrepresented communities in their syllabi and revise them or acknowledge with students the significance of the exclusion of those voices in their fields as a limitation. I have incorporated this into my own practice as an administrator.

Both the Atlantic and Polytech honors colleges had student organizations to engage honors students outside the classroom. But at both institutions, students described honors as lacking community among students of color. As they reflected on "being the only one" in their majors or academic programs, it was also hard for them to identify other Black women (or any students of color) who were in honors. Honors colleges could address this concern by creating intentional opportunities through programming for students to gather based on their academic or social affinity and facilitating more networking opportunities. Building a network among Black students can help play a role in building that sense of community and coping with environmental challenges (Grier-Reed, 2013; Winkle-Wagner et al., 2019; Byrd & Porter, 2022). Black women need nurturing environments—designed to address their distinctive multifaceted identities and needs to help realize their potential (Gold, 2011; Commodore, Baker, & Arroyo, 2018; Patton & Croom, 2017). While student connections with Black faculty and staff remain essential to fostering an environment of support, it is important for the university and honors colleges not to place an additional onus on Black people alone. Creating an inclusive environment for high-achieving Black women, and students of diverse backgrounds more broadly, is the responsibility of all university professionals, consistent with the values of the institution (Porter, 2017; Davis, 2018). In addition to helping remove barriers to these students' success, universities should educate all students and professionals about stereotypes and implicit bias and teach them how to overcome oppressive systems (Winkle-Wagner et al., 2019; Steele, 2022). Each of these actionable strategies would enable universities to make campuses safer and more supportive for high-achieving Black women.

Expanding the Research

In order to include underrepresented populations, particularly at PWIs, high-achievement ability should not be characterized solely by students' performance in the classroom. Community involvement, employment, demonstrated leadership in student organizations, and recommendations describing the student's growth and potential were also important factors in determining a student's ability to achieve. This research began a dialogue with the extant literature to redefine what it labels a high-achieving undergraduate and shift the focus from test scores to more holistic evaluations of students' ability to be successful at college. As the barriers to college access posed by standardized testing were continually scrutinized, the test-optional admissions movement has gained momentum, suggesting that more universities and honors colleges reconsider the criteria they used to admit students. The shift to more holistic selection measures offered hope for enhanced inclusion for Black women and other students of color as well as an important topic of study in higher education.

The array of definitions that students used for their academic identities reiterated the idea that the terms gifted, high-achieving, and honors need revisiting. More research, both qualitative and quantitative, was needed on academically talented students to better understand them more broadly and also more specifically, through exploring the many minoritized subgroups (low-income, first-generation, or immigrant students) among them. Future research should focus on a more diverse set of honors or academically talented students from varying age groups—such as nontraditional older and younger college students—and those attending community colleges and historically Black institutions. Examining this population with consideration of the within-group diversity among honors students and Black women would offer a more robust understanding of who they are and how they process their collegiate experience.

Participation in an honors college was one way to provide support for academically talented students, but there were others that also warrant attention. Talented Black women also attend highly selective institutions and participate in medical scholars programs. A longitudinal or ethnographic project to gain deeper clarity about the experiences and salience of identities of high-achieving undergraduate Black women would also contribute greatly to the literature. With the support of more research on these brilliant students, practitioners can revise terminology—here I advocated for incorporating academically talented into the discourse—and inform admissions policies and student services that foster inclusivity and the appropriate kinds of support.

Conclusion

To ensure that Black high-achieving undergraduate women have the tools to become successful in college and remain so in society, universities need to enhance campus resources for them. Imagine all that academically talented Black women could accomplish if there were no threats to their self-expression at college. Consider the kinds of contributions they could make as professionals if they felt more supported in their classrooms and more welcomed among their peers. Consider if there were no judgments on their expressions of brilliance. Honors colleges are only one way to enhance the social capital of and provide a more engaging academic experience for this population. There are potentially many more ways to accomplish this, using what is known about the perspectives of these students.

By sharing their experiences inside and outside the classroom, the participants in this study shed light on their lived reality that being Black women, specifically Black high-achievers, is more than just the sum of the parts of the participants' identities. They live at the nexus of their mutually influential identities, a unique intersection of minoritized social groups that is often invisible in the research, the literature, on campus, and in society. Making the most of the support they received from faculty and staff, and carefully traversing the challenges present in those same contexts, enabled the students to be academically successful at institutions where most people did not share their identities. No student should have to endure such obstacles in their pursuit of success. Despite the messages society or campus life may send them, this research and the resilient Black high-achieving undergraduate women living in resistance at its center are proof that students like them could and should be Black and smart.

Academically talented Black undergraduate women are not oxymorons nor contradictions nor anomalies. They are not magical, and their experiences are real. They are future doctors, educators, and lawyers. They will be nurses, engineers, social workers, and other contributors to society. Like other students, they are people with the need to feel supported, seen, validated, and welcomed in their communities. Brilliant Black women like the ones I interviewed exist on every college campus, but as underrepresented students at PWIs, they are commonly overlooked, ignored, or silenced. They are isolated and lack the freedom to express their authentic selves. Historical stereotypical roles are projected at them from every direction. They are the only one, the default educator, the angry Black woman, and the superwoman achiever. But Black women high-achievers are talented and capable; they simply need the support to achieve their full potential and accomplish great things academically and beyond.

The high-achieving Black women featured in this book are just like some of the students on every college campus in the United States. They used the strategies and skills they were taught and gleaned along the way to traverse the sometimes-treacherous landscape of college life. All universities have a duty to foster environments that help high-achieving Black women students thrive. College life can be threatening, or it can foster a level of confidence that will help students achieve more than they imagine is possible. Armed with this insight into their lives, seek out the voices of these talented students and listen. Give them your attention. Hear about their obstacles and triumphs through the everyday challenges of college life. Let their testimonies recolor your impressions about whom and what smart could be. Academically talented Black women deserve the opportunity to soar on campus and beyond as their authentic, brilliant selves.

Acknowledgments

Thanks to my students, past and present, who sparked the fire to do this work.

Thanks to my mentor, colleague, friend, and committee chair, Dr. James Earl Davis, for guidance with all the iterations of this project. Thanks for dreaming about the possibilities for this work.

Additional thanks to Dr. Will Jordan, Dr. Catherine Schifter, and Dr. Sharon Fries-Britt for serving on my dissertation committee. Gratitude to my critical friend Dr. Martha Carey for the friendship, editing, and providing virtual support in countless other ways during the research process and the creation of this book project. And thanks to Team Honors for never letting me be the smartest person in the room.

To my family: Jay and Raven and Ella and Miles. My greatest appreciation for their unwavering confidence in my ability to achieve—despite my own doubts and the challenges outside of my control—and giving me the courage to do more than I thought possible.

Appendix

Research Methods

This study used qualitative research methods to examine the experiences of high-achieving Black undergraduate women inside and outside the classroom. This section discusses the design and findings from the pilot study and outlines the study including the research site, participants, and data collection and analysis methods.

I conducted a study on high-achieving Black women using data from undergraduates in the honors college at Atlantic University, a large, urban, predominantly White research institution. This pilot study addressed two research questions: What were the experiences of Black high-achieving college students inside and outside the classroom at a predominantly White urban university, and which aspects of their identity were most salient to the meaning high-achieving Black women attributed to their experiences in college? Participants were recruited using a targeted email to students of color in the honors program and group Facebook posts to members of associated student organizations. After obtaining their consent, I verified the participants' membership in the program and determined their current GPA in consult with honors staff, based on students' academic records. After completing an electronic background questionnaire, I conducted semistructured interviews in person at the campus library. Interviews were audio recorded and transcribed to aid data analysis.

The purpose of the pilot was to test the data collection instruments, specifically to determine if the information students shared in their responses about their personal identity and experiences effectively addressed the research questions based on the protocol prompts. Eight interviews were conducted, but due to complications with one of the audio recordings, one interview did not have a complete transcription. Reflecting on my experience with the pilot study, I made the most of this opportunity to examine and improve my approach as a researcher and anticipate adjustments that were needed for the study.

The process of the pilot study was very informative for both the interview protocol and the exploration of common issues among this population on campus. Although students indicated that they understood the questions, there were a few lines of questioning on identity about which students consistently requested clarification. Those questions were reworked and the sections were consolidated to improve the flow of interviews for the next study.

Data analysis for the pilot was an iterative process that occurred during and after the data collection phase of the study. I incorporated Seidman's (2006) approach to analyzing interview data by creating a participant profile after each interview that included their responses to the background questionnaire and my observations from our interaction. Transcripts from each interview were closely read, and I created memos to track themes in the experiences across the interviews. Basic ideas and information from each passage were classified into codes. After coding a few interviews, I consolidated similar codes and proceeded to code the remaining interviews using a consistent code tree. Codes were sorted into categories and then into concepts or themes that were significant to the topic of interest: the intersectionality of issues of gender, race, and high-achievement status.

A few themes emerged from the interviews: (1) women in this study were commonly the only person of color in their classes with other high-achievers, (2) tension existed among their performance and perceptions of their intersecting identities of being smart Black women, particularly in their social interactions with peers, and (3) racialized and gendered experiences were subtle inside the classroom but overt in other environments. Overall, findings from the pilot confirmed my expectation that high-achieving Black undergraduate women faced personal, interpersonal, and structural challenges in several areas of campus life as a result of their intersecting identities. This study shed light on those obstacles, the strategies women in this group used to overcome them, and argued the importance of addressing the unique needs of the students in this population at PWIs.

The purpose of the present study was to understand how academically talented Black undergraduate women overcome the challenges in their college experience. Two research questions guided this study: (1) What were the experiences of Black high-achieving college women inside and outside of the classroom at a predominantly White university? and (2) Which aspects of their identity were most salient to the meaning high-achieving Black women attributed to their experiences in college? The open-ended and exploratory nature of the research questions made qualitative methods the most appropriate approach to understanding the experiences of the women in the study. Qualitative methods examine how people make meaning around their life experiences, interactions, or discourse in their everyday lives (Lichtman, 2010; Bogdan & Biklen, 1982). This method addressed how and why questions and operated from the assumption that knowledge was socially constructed and subjective: that diverse participants had varying experiences that shaped their perspectives and realities (Lichtman, 2010; Teddlie & Tashakkori, 2009).

The qualitative researcher is her own research tool; as such, I interacted with participants to collect data and engage in an interpretive process to determine how they understand the nature of their identities and how they overcome the challenges they face as undergraduates (Creswell, 2009). Recognizing that my context as a researcher was central to the interpretive lens used to understand the students' experiences, consistent with the practices of qualitative inquiry, I aimed to position the participants as the experts in order to allow them to share their own voices in the research (Denzin & Giardina, 2007; Lichtman, 2010). This qualitative approach illustrated the complexity of the challenges this group of high-achieving Black undergraduate women experienced by addressing the many layers of those challenges.

Data Sources and Collection

The full process of gaining access and data collection took from spring 2015 though summer 2016. Before beginning the study, I obtained prior approval from the dean of the honors college at Polytech University in late spring 2015 semester, which was submitted as part of the Institutional Review Board (IRB) approval process for my institution to verify approval for me to conduct the study. This also verified the college's agreement to help with disseminating the call for participants via targeted emails to the population of interest.

Data were collected using a number of sources, including in-person interviews, background questionnaire responses, and descriptive university statistics. The selection of these particular methods was informed by the qualitative interpretivist nature of the research questions and the intersectional theoretical perspective that shaped the approach to this study

(Hesse-Biber & Leavy, 2011). All of the data collection tools below were submitted at my institution and to the IRB at Atlantic University and Polytech University for approval prior to the collection of any data.

CAMPUS AND HONORS COLLEGE
DEMOGRAPHIC DATA

This information was obtained from the Honors College staff at both institutions, the Atlantic University and Polytech University institutional research offices, and the Integrated Postsecondary Education Data System (IPEDS) from the National Center for Education Statistics website.

Background Questionnaire. Prior to in-person interviews, participants shared their background information via a private (electronic) Google Form. This document collected information associated with students' personal academic achievement (e.g., high school and college GPA), goals (e.g., highest degree planned and career goals), socioeconomic status (e.g., household income, parent educational attainment), and self-defined racial identity. These criteria were included in the questionnaire to allow the in-person interviews to focus more deeply on students' perceptions about their identity and specific experiences instead of the collection of basic demographic data.

Interviews. A semistructured interview was conducted with the dean of the Polytech honors college prior to interviewing undergraduates. This interview focused on learning about the culture of the honors college, the faculty and staff that work with honors students, and a general understanding about the history of the college and its context at the university.

Although it was anticipated that data collection would begin in summer 2015, infrequent and insufficient contact with the site coordinator at Polytech led to significant delays in the call for participants' email. At the end of the fall 2015 term, only five subjects had responded to the background questionnaire, and only two completed interviews or responded to my communication. Due to the poor response rate at Polytech, another call for participants was issued at Atlantic University at the start of spring 2016. Data collection was more fruitful at Atlantic and proceeded through the end of the semester.

A purposive sample of students was selected from individuals who responded to a call for participation via email from the staff of the honors college at each university. Sixteen students completed both the online background questionnaire and individual, semistructured, in-person interviews between fall 2015 and spring 2016. Participants shared their availability for interviews as part of the background questionnaire. I communicated with each participant to coordinate an interview based on their availability at an on- or off-campus location of their preference. Interviews lasted sixty to seventy-five minutes, were audio recorded, and were transcribed for analysis. Second interviews, which were also in person, served as member checks and a follow-up to discuss themes from across the first interviews. They lasted forty-five to sixty minutes.

Particular areas of focus for the student interviews were (1) how high-achieving Black women perceive the importance of the various aspects of their identities in their social interactions in campus life and (2) how their perceptions of their own experiences in campus life reflected their identities. Examination of those two ideas provided indications of the ways systems of power in society were operative in campus life.

Periodic memos. I also used periodic memos during the data collection and analysis process to track my reactions to students' responses, the emergence of themes, or any other notable observations. I incorporated the approach used by

Harper and Quaye's study as a model by writing memos or a "textural summary" for each participant to help me track "*what* each high-achiever experienced" and "*how* [she] experienced the phenomenon" respectively of being an academically talented student at a PWI (Harper & Quaye, 2007, p. 133). This process facilitated a streamlined process from examining similarities or differences among participants in an accessible format.

Data Analysis

Data analysis was iterative and occurred during and after the data collection period of the study. Descriptive data about the site population and the participant demographics were analyzed as soon as they were available. This information included socioeconomic background, academic major, academic and professional goals, and self-defined ethnic and racial identities as indicated in the background questionnaire responses. Analysis of the interview transcripts, the composition of analytical memos, and preliminary coding were all ongoing during the study.

Prior to the start of student interviews, a provisional list of eighteen codes were created based on the research questions and theoretical framework shaping the study. As the major source of data, interviews were transcribed and read closely to identify important ideas. Categories of codes were also created based on the sections of the interview protocol, including relationships with family and friends, high-achieving term definitions, performance of identity, classroom and social experiences, and aspirations. Memos, bracketed reactions in the transcripts, textural and structural summaries (Harper & Quaye, 2007), and participant profiles (Seidman, 2006) were used to help with early examination of additional important ideas in the data. I expanded the code list while closely reading and annotating all of the data, end-ing with seventy-eight codes. Categories of codes were revised based on the significant concepts in the transcript data, then combined to identify common themes across the students' experiences (Miles & Huberman, 1994). Narrative quotes or chunks from the transcriptions were classified by classroom or social context and around major concepts of the intersectionality theoretical perspective; separate files were created for each concept and associated data were collected using reports in ATLAS.ti to analyze evidence supporting those concepts (Seidman, 2006). Comprehensive analysis of all data collected during the study occurred during the summer and fall after the completion of the data collection phase, during which the bulk of writing occurred. There were ninety-seven codes in the final codebook, inclusive of thematic supercodes used for Atlas.ti searches.

Validity and Trustworthiness

Asking Black women to speak for themselves was the best way to learn more about their experiences. The selection of qualitative interviews for the data collection method privileged these women's perspectives, providing them an opportunity to contribute their voices to the discourse on the college experience. Methodologically, the decision to consider the experiences of these students without a comparison group was to make their experiences central to the study. These experiences were valuable as sources without the need for comparison against a White or male normative group (West, Donovan, & Roemer, 2009).

Reliability of the study procedures and the findings were supported in a variety of ways. Using the criteria outlined by Miles and Huberman (1994) as a guide, the present study addressed my positionality in the site, connected findings to the data and the intersectional theoretical framework, and used coding checks to ensure dependability of the research. As part of the data analysis process, a colleague reviewed the code book to ensure there was clarity in the coding scheme and that it was consistent with the research questions and interview protocol for the study. This inter-rater review served as an indicator of the fit and directness of explanations of the coding scheme for the data (Miles & Huberman, 1994). The result of the intercoder check revealed a number of redundancies and overly detailed codes that did not directly address the focus of the study. Due to the differences in perceived code necessity, where appropriate, I consolidated a number of codes and clarified their parameters for application to better explain how various passages were labeled with each code.

Internal validity of the study and the data was supported by member checks. After student in-person interviews, I met with each participant in person to review the transcript of the communication and give her an opportunity to review what she shared with me. This review meeting gave the student time to reflect on the interview and consider if there were areas of discussion on which she wanted to elaborate or for which she wanted to clarify what she shared. Including the participant in this stage of the data analysis and verification enhanced her trust of the research process and ensured that the participant would feel the interview was an accurate representation of her own experiences. I also used this time to follow up on questions that were not fully addressed in the initial interview and seek clarification of areas of uncertainty (Miles & Huberman, 1994).

External validity for the present study was primarily theoretical; the small sample of students in this population prevents generalizability to "other actual contexts," but the participants' experiences were particularly instrumental for considering the kinds of challenges that similar groups of students could face in similar contexts (Miles & Huberman, 1994). The intersectional theoretical framework supports this validity by uncovering the ways that systems of power function to oppress high-achieving Black women undergraduates in their interactions with others in academic and campus life. These same forces were functions of society and may be similarly operative in other social contexts as well.

In the pilot study, students' active status in honors was verified using access to student records from members of the honors college. In order to protect the confidentiality of the students and their choice to participate in the study, students' information was not verified with the staff in either honors college. Therefore, I had to trust that the respondents provided accurate data regarding their academic achievement information such as GPA, majors, and good standing in honors at the time of the study.

Ethical Considerations

In order to respect the privacy of the students and the honors college, the names of the participants and the site were kept confidential. All students were assigned pseudonyms in the transcriptions and final report in order to protect their identities. Each participant completed an informed consent form electronically before the background questionnaire and also before the start of the in-person interviews and had the opportunity to choose not to proceed in the study. I respected the confidentiality of each participant in the study, keeping any identifying information and their responses private and in a locked storage unit in my home office. Electronic responses were kept in a password-protected file.

As expressed in the previous section, I recognized the importance of maintaining the confidentiality of individual students' participation in the study from the honors college staff. This consideration of anonymity for the students supported their trust in me as a researcher and hopefully encouraged them to feel that they could be open and honest in our interviews. I reviewed the informed consent form with them and also obtained their written consent at the start of the first in-person interview. They kept a copy for their records, and so they had my contact information if needed. They also had the opportunity to do a member check once the interview was transcribed, which provided them with an opportunity to ask any questions about the study in person.

The professional staff at Polytech University were receptive to my study, but I was still cognizant of the importance of taking time to build trust with them since I was an outsider and was employed at a neighboring institution with a similar population and may be viewed as a competitor. I viewed my administrative role as a benefit to the study procedures as well as to the honors college as I had experience working with this population, and my pilot study helped me anticipate potential personal and ethical challenges to the research.

Limitations

Qualitative research studies focus on depth of examination over breadth; therefore the results of this study are not generalizable to nor necessarily representative of the broader population of all high-achieving Black women in college nationally. Limitations of the interview data collection method include the number of participants, depth over breadth, and the reliance on the researcher as the data collection tool. Learning about students' experiences inside and outside the classroom in two sixty- to seventy-five-minute semistructured interviews cannot create a holistic illustration of the students' overall experience overcoming a variety of challenges in college. In addition, data collection took about eight months, and this short time in the field is also a limitation. More interviews of a longer length and unstructured nature with more students might produce deeper insight; however, as with all studies, there is a limited timeline and no perfect research tool. The method for this study creates a snapshot of the students' experiences and uses a sample of students from across academic years.

As discussed in earlier sections, using honors college affiliation as a proxy for high-achieving status remains problematic. There are Black women at Atlantic University and Polytech University that are not part of the honors colleges but whose collegiate academic performance and involvement would indicate that they could be labeled high-achieving. If honors were defined more inclusively—through applying Harper and Quaye's focus (2007) on character and community involvement, for example—they might have been eligible for the study, but extant criteria preclude them from potential participation.

PURPOSE OF THE STUDY AND RESEARCH QUESTIONS

The purpose of this book was to understand how academically talented Black undergraduate women overcome the challenges in their college experience. Through this research, I aimed to contribute to the limited empirical research on high-achieving students and break the color and gender barriers in the literature by focusing on Black women. Two questions guided this research:

What were the experiences of Black high-achieving college women inside and outside the classroom at a predominantly White university?

Which aspects of their identity were most salient to the meaning high-achieving Black women attributed to their experiences in college?

A large part of undergraduate life was spent in the class-room, but how students chose to spend their time outside of it also played an important role in their college experience. Informal interactions with faculty and staff, involvement in student organizations, and other engagement within the campus or local communities all impact students' experiences (Pascarella & Terenzini, 2005). By considering these students holistically—their academic and social contexts in addition to their ethnic and gender identities—this book helps iden-tify some of the unique needs of this population, which will enable administrators to craft the specific services needed to support them (Fries-Britt & Griffin, 2007).

Significance of the Study

Understanding the experiences of high-achieving Black women was an important yet often overlooked part of fos-tering student success in college, particularly at PWIs. The emergence of studies in higher education on undergraduates of color over the last fifteen years focused on the experiences of Black men of a variety of ability types, expanding the knowledge on that population (Cuyjet, 2006; Harper, 2005; Harper & Quaye, 2007; Pearson & Kohl, 2010; Strayhorn, 2009; Wood & Palmer, 2015; Palmer, Wood & Arroyo, 2015). From that body of research came valuable information about how to enhance the academic environment for Black men (Bonner & Bailey, 2006), best practices for specific inter-ventions that support the needs of Black men through men-toring or community-building organizations (Bledsoe & Rome, 2006; Baker, 2006), and patterns and outcomes of their engagement in campus life (Harper, 2005; Strayhorn & DeVita, 2010; Harper & Quaye, 2007). For example, according to Comeaux (2013), "Black male collegians' campus involvement is often time grossly diminished because of an oppressive and discriminatory campus climate influence and perpetuated by significant members of the college community," one that can discourage their participation socially or academically (p. 454). Although these studies made major contributions, there was a general lack of similar research on Black women, especially high-achievers.

Recent additions to the literature on Black women were detailed in chapter 2 and featured significant developments focused on social homogeneity, isolation, lack of good mentoring relationships, mental health stress, and affording college (Commodore, Baker, & Arroyo, 2018). Another edited volume on Black women and college success also addressed historical and generational perspectives, identity politics, and Black women attending an Ivy League school (Stewart, 2017; Porter, 2017; Shaw, 2017; Johnson, 2017).

Studies showed that environments at PWIs posed several challenges to students of color; spaces could be experienced differently by different people with membership to a variety of group identities (Steele, 2010). For Black high-achieving women, their position at the intersection of multiple oppressions played a role in how they made meaning around college life. Campus life mirrored the patterns of racial organization in greater society through its "racial marginalization, racial segregation of social and academic networks" and underrepresentation inside and outside the classroom by faculty and university staff (Steele, 2010, p. 26); as such, there needed to be more attention paid to the meaning that high-achieving Black women perceived their various identities had in those contexts. This book examined how salient various identities were to high-achieving Black women in college individually and collectively, revealing the ways institutional oppression functioned at PWIs and in social interactions on and off campus.

An examination of the experiences of high-achieving under-graduate Black women required attention to the complexity of the identities that made them subject to multiple oppressions (Collins, 1991). The ethnic and gender identities, among others, had sociopolitical and historical connotations within the larger context of American society for this population of Black women. As microcosms of U.S. society, college campuses were sites where the systems of power that subordinate these students as women, as Black, and by class, also manifested in the interactions that occur as part of campus life (Banks, 2009; Commodore, Baker, & Arroyo, 2018). The present study employed a framework that facilitated the analysis of these aspects of identity and power constructs based on the lived experiences of the women at the center of this research.

Intersectionality was an instrumental "interpretive framework for thinking through how intersections of race and class, or race and gender, or sexuality and class, for example, shape any group's experience across specific social contexts" (Collins, 1998, p. 208). With its roots in the work of law scholar Kimberlé Williams Crenshaw (1989, 1991) and Black feminist scholar Patricia Hill Collins (1991), this perspective historically focused "attention on the vexed dynamics of difference and the solidarities of sameness in the context of antidiscrimination and social movement politics" (Cho, Crenshaw, & McCall, 2013). It was a tool used to advocate for the incorporation of "race-, class-, and gender-inclusive interpretations" of the lived experiences of women of color in sociological and legal discourse and research (Collins, 1998, p. 205). In its early applications, intersectionality was a "content-based specialization that emphasized the subjectivity of women who reside at the intersections of race-, gender-, class-, and sexual orientation-based marginalization (and other categories of difference)" (Hancock, 2007, p. 248). Over time, its reach expanded from Black feminist thought to critical race to educational and political science examinations of difference, taking on the attributes of a theoretical approach (Cho et al., 2013). Collins (1998) described the framework as follows: "As a heuristic device, intersectionality references the ability of social phenomena such as race, class, and gender to mutually construct one another . . . [it can be used to] think through social institutions, organizational structures, patterns of social interactions, and other social practices on all levels of social organization" (p. 205).

This study recognized Black women as "agents of knowledge" by examining the experiences of Black women from their own words and personal experiences to learn about them individually and as a group within society (Collins, 1998, p. 177). The intersectional framework did not inherently privilege one aspect of identity over the others; however, it recognized that their "salience varies among and within groups" (Collins, 1998, p. 208) and that the analyses of power in various contexts served to "reveal which differences carry significance" (Tomlinson, 2013, as found in Cho et al., 2013, p. 798). As such, the study shed light on how inextricable students perceived these aspects of their identities and how these influenced the ways they saw the world, and in turn, how the world viewed them. Patterns of social interactions as evidenced in the specific racialized and gendered situations that students shared in their in-person interviews aided in the analysis of power dynamics for women in this population individually and as a social group on campus.

Approaches that considered each of the factors of Black women's identities independently or in binary relationships ignored the ways in which these facets build upon each other, which is essential to understanding the meaning these women make around their experiences (Collins, 1998; Collins, 2015). Centering this study on the more inclusive analysis of the lived experiences of women of color was one of the trademark contributions of this analytical method. This book considers the "multiple axes" of gender and race within the social contexts of campus life for academically talented college students in a holistic way, an approach not taken in previous studies. This population had also not been considered in previous intersectional studies. A deeper discussion of the assumptions associated with intersectionality and notable studies are included in chapter 2.

RESEARCH SITES: POLYTECH UNIVERSITY AND ATLANTIC UNIVERSITY

One site for the study was Polytech University, a private urban research institution located near the city's bustling downtown commerce area and bordering a neighborhood with high property values. It is a doctorate-granting, has a high research activity university Carnegie Classification, and has about two hundred academic degree programs and fifteen academic colleges. It was founded in the late 1800s and has a reputation for its highly selective science, technology, engineering, and math (STEM) programs as well as its focus on experiential learning. According to its website, there were about seventeen thousand undergraduates as of fall 2015. Nearly half of undergraduates were from out of state and about 15 percent were international students. The university was predominantly White (56 percent); the rest of the undergraduate population was 13 percent international, 12 percent Asian, 7 percent Black/African American, and 6 percent Hispanic/Latino students. Multiracial students represented 3 percent of undergraduates, and 3 percent of students' ethnicities were unknown.

The Honors College at Polytech

The honors college was created in the early 1990s and featured a small community of students from across the university's majors. It represented the university's commitment to invest in its most promising students seeking an enhanced learning experience at college. Its mission was to enhance the intellectual and experiential aspects of high-achieving college students' experience at Polytech University through its offerings of unique opportunities and personalized advising. The college supported students in their pursuit of academic engagement and social involvement.

All applications to Polytech University were evaluated for admission to the honors college. Exceptional students that were admitted to Polytech University were invited to participate in the college as part of their admissions package. Incoming and current students, including transfer students, were also able to apply directly to the honors college for admission. All prospective students were evaluated based on their high school academic record, standardized test scores, extracurricular involvement, and demonstrated leadership potential. According to honors website, qualified current student applicants had at least a 3.75 GPA, demonstrated a record of engagement in campus and community life, and positive student conduct.

In order to earn the honors college notation on their academic transcript, students had to complete all of the course and experiential requirements and maintain at least a 3.2 GPA (3.5 for distinction status). During their time at the university, students maintained their good standing in the college by completing a series of honors courses and colloquia. As upperclassmen, they were required to complete experiential learning projects, such as independent studies or major or career-related practical experiences. Students that failed to make progress in the areas of GPA or course or experiential requirements could be dismissed from the program. Some of the benefits of honors college membership included access to dedicated study and residential community spaces, unique leadership opportunities in honors student organizations, discussion-oriented classes with low student-faculty ratios, and support from honors staff. Honors students also had priority course registration, and after completing the program requirements could earn distinction status upon graduation.

Atlantic Honors College

The pilot study site, Atlantic University, served as the second site for the study. All of the Atlantic participants were full-time undergraduates at the state-affiliated urban research university. Atlantic was moderately selective, granted doctorates, was a high research activity university Carnegie Classification, and had about 450 academic degree programs, including 150 undergraduate programs across 13 academic colleges. It was also founded in the late 1800s, with the purpose of providing educational opportunities for the city's working class. A low-income housing project and homes with lower property value neighbored the campus.

According to its website, there were about twenty-eight thousand undergraduates as of fall 2015. Most students were in-state, with less than 25 percent of undergraduates from out of state and about 6 percent international students. The university was predominantly White (56 percent); the rest of the undergraduate population was less than 1 percent American Indian or Pacific Islander, 6 percent international, 10 percent Asian, 13 percent Black/African American, and

6 percent Hispanic/Latino students. Multiracial students represented 3 percent of undergraduates and 6 percent of students' ethnicities were unknown. At the time of the study, there were about two thousand honors students. Black women made up less than 15 percent of full-time undergraduates and only about 3 percent of the honors population.

Atlantic Honors College Requirements. All incoming freshmen were evaluated based on the overall strength of their application to the university for admission to the honors college, like Polytech admits. Although Atlantic was less selective than Polytech, recent enhancements to the merit aid levels made the university more attractive to academically talented prospective students. Students whom the admissions office awarded the highest level of merit scholarship were automatically admitted to honors, and most of those at the second tier were admitted to the honors college as part of their admissions package. Current Atlantic students and transfers could apply directly to the honors college during the academic year via the College's webpage, which included short answer questions about the student's interests, plans for taking honors courses, and research. According to the staff, qualified current student applicants had at least a 3.7 GPA, though most admits were higher.

To graduate from the honors college, students needed to complete at least ten honors courses and maintain a 3.25 cumulative GPA. Four of those courses had to be at an advanced level. Courses were offered across the university curriculum with most concentrated in liberal arts, the sciences, and business, which were the most popular colleges among honors students. Students whose GPA fell below 3.25 or did not progress with coursework were dismissed from the college but were offered the opportunity to return if they could bring their GPA back up to the required level.

Participants

A purposive sample of students was selected from individuals who responded to a call for participation via email from the staff of the honors college at Polytechnic University or Atlantic University. Of the twenty-one students that submitted the background questionnaire, sixteen people completed both the online background questionnaire and participated in in-person interviews. All participants in the study were full-time undergraduate, traditional-age women affiliated with the honors college at Polytech or Atlantic University. For this study, membership in the honors college denoted high-achievement status. Students were selected based on their race or ethnicity as indicated on the background questionnaire. All the participants self-identified with racial identities, which included African American or Black. Half of the participants were first-generation Americans whose parents immigrated from the West Indies or West Africa. All the participants considered themselves at least partially American-identified, and each came of age in the United States.

There were few differences between the students from the two sites. Aside from the strong likelihood for Polytech students to major in science or technology (STEM), the students were comparable in their family and other background criteria. As such, this study analyzed the data from all the students together—since the students' experiences were the focus and not their honors colleges—but kept the differences in institutional contexts in mind during data analysis.

Academic Programs

Participants varied in their class year, academic field of study, and anticipated career fields. Table 1 displays the participant

TABLE 1. Participant Demographics

NAME	AGE	CLASS YEAR	FIELD OF STUDY
Anissa	17	Freshman	STEM
Lauryn	18	Freshman	Health professions
Grace	18	Freshman	Arts
Shantel	18	Freshman	Social sciences
Aisha	18	Freshman	Health professions
Mia	19	Freshman	Health professions
Keshia	19	Sophomore	Health professions
Zoe	19	Sophomore	Humanities
Crystal	19	Sophomore	STEM
Michelle	19	Sophomore	Health professions
Amber	19	Sophomore	Social sciences
Serena	19	Sophomore	STEM
Miranda	20	Junior	Social sciences
Nicole	20	Junior	Business
Jacqueline	21	Senior	Arts
Shannon	23	Senior	STEM

demographic information including age, class year, and the field of study.

Students in the study were all traditional-age college students, ranging from seventeen to twenty-two years old. There were first-semester freshmen through seniors, and all but one anticipated graduating within four years. The fifth-year senior was pleased with her extra time at the college as it afforded her more than one full-term internship for academic credit. Most of the students were freshmen or sophomores. Many of the students also mentioned taking Advanced Placement courses in high school to earn prior credits for college.

Students majored in academic disciplines across the humanities to STEM to business, as illustrated in table 1. STEM majors included computer and information sciences and biology. Health professions included public health, nursing, and communications science and disorders majors. Humanities and social sciences included English, political science, and sociology. Arts included music and design majors. Ten of the students were also enrolled in certificate, minor or preprofessional tracks. Their average GPA was a 3.6 on a 4.0 scale.

Nearly all of the students planned to pursue additional degrees after completing college. Only one seemed concerned about her ability to finish college, citing her high financial need and the understanding that extenuating circumstances could arise to get her off track. Despite any challenges, she still planned to pursue graduate studies. The one student unsure of her postgraduate plans felt that more formal education was not a necessity to progress in her industry. Students had high academic aspirations. Half planned to earn a master's degree, while the remaining students anticipated some form of doctorate, including medical and law degrees. Participants were aspiring epidemiologists, nurses and pediatricians, designers, lawyers, military and government officials, IT consultants, financial analysts, authors, and music producers.

Family Background

The background questionnaire inquired about parents, their educational completion, and family income. All of the students listed their guardians as their mother and father. One participant indicated her mother was the only parent but shared some information about her father during her interview. Nearly all of the students were co-parented, though a few had parents who were divorced or remarried. Most of the students had siblings, some of whom had attended or anticipated going to college as well.

Table 2 illustrates estimated family income and parents' degree completion. As the background data were self-reported, the income levels may be inaccurate. According to data from the Pew Charitable Trust Foundation on middle-class income levels for a nearby state, none of the participants were from below middle class (Kane & Keirsz, 2015). All of

TABLE 2. Family Education and Income Levels

HIGHEST LEVEL EDUCATION: PARENT/ GUARDIAN #1	PARENT/ GUARDIAN #1	HIGHEST LEVEL EDUCATION: PARENT/ GUARDIAN #2	PARENT/ GUARDIAN #2	ESTIMATED ANNUAL FAMILY INCOME
Associate's or technical degree	Mother	GED	Father	$30,000—$49,999
Bachelor's degree	Mother	Master's degree	Father	$30,000—$49,999
High school diploma	Mother	Some college	Father	$30,000—$49,999
Some college	Mother	Some college	Father	$30,000—$49,999
Some college	Mother	Bachelor's degree	Father	$50,000—$99,999
Associate's or technical degree	Mom	High school diploma	Dad	$50,000—$99,999
Bachelor's degree	Mother	Master's degree	Father	$50,000—$99,999
Master's degree	Mother	Master's degree	Father	Above $100,000
Bachelor's degree	Mother	Master's degree	Father	Above $100,000
Master's degree	Mother	Bachelor's degree	Father	Above $100,000
Master's degree	Mother	Bachelor's degree	Father	Above $100,000
Master's degree	Mother	Bachelor's degree	Father	Above $100,000
Bachelor's, pursuing master's	Mother	n/a	n/a	Above $100,000
Bachelor's degree	Mother	Master's degree	Father	Above $100,000
Master's degree	Mother	Master's degree	Father	Above $100,000
Master's degree	Mother	Some college	Father	Above $100,000

the participants were from families earning above $30,000 per year. About 25 percent were lower middle class, another 25 percent were in the middle, and the remaining 50 percent were upper middle class or higher, earning more than $100,000 per year. Another marker of social class and economic background was the students' discussion of their employment during college. Among the four students that indicated they had jobs during the academic year, only one mentioned working more than twenty hours per week: that same student was not in any student groups. The other employed students worked between fifteen and twenty hours per week and used their funds to supplement their college costs. Their families or merit-based, financial, or other funding sources covered most of their major expenses. Most mentioned internships or summer jobs to save money for the academic year.

None of the students were first-generation college students, but two would be among the first in their family to pursue a traditional four-year education. Some of the parents completed associate's degrees or technical programs at other kinds of institutions. Four of the participants would be the first generation to successfully complete a bachelor's degree: some of the parents had attended but not completed college. Overall, participants were from solvent, middle-class, relatively educated families.

Students were raised primarily in the United States; two had spent some time growing up abroad in Europe and the Middle East. Nearly half of the students were the children of immigrants; all but one of the participants were born in the United States. The families of the first-generation Americans were predominantly from West Africa and the Caribbean, including Nigeria, Ghana, Trinidad, and Cameroon. The prominence of students from immigrant families among this small group of high-achievers was reflective of their burgeoning population in the United States and at American universities in recent years, particularly at elite institutions (Massey et al., 2007; Mwangi & Fries-Britt, 2015). Since all of the participants came of age in the United States, I anticipated that their acculturation reflected an understanding of and immersion in United States social practices prior to college. American society may force people of different nationalities into the same racial group in the United States, but the reality was that there could be stark differences in understanding among people who were socialized with American customs and social attitudes from those who were socialized elsewhere with a different set of norms and cultural contexts. With the prominence of immigrant families among the participants, however, I understood that values associated with their nationality and ethnicity played an important role in the students' experiences. As noted by Mwangi and Fries-Britt, "Black immigrants often experience issues of race, racism, and discrimination in ways different from Black Americans and non-Black immigrants" (2015, p.18). Those differences play a role in their adjustment to and experiences within campus life. No international students applied for the study, but if they had, they would not have been eligible participants because of the anticipated differences in their socialization from other participants.

Notes

Chapter 1   Students Like Jada

1. Collins, P. H. (1991/2000). *Black feminist thought: Knowledge, consciousness, and the politics of empowerment*. Routledge, p. 33.

Chapter 3   Learning while Black and Brilliant

Epigraph: hooks, b. (2014). *Teaching to transgress education as the practice of freedom*. Taylor and Francis. https://doi.org/10.4324/9780203700280

Chapter 5   Performing Authentic Identities

Epigraph: Williamson, M. (1996). *A return to love: Reflections on the principles of a course in miracles*. HarperCollins.

References

Anderson, G. (2019, September 24). InsideHigherEd.com. Minority and first-generation SAT scores fall behind. Retrieved December 9, 2020, from https://www.insidehighered.com/admissions/article/2019/09/24/minority-and-first-generation-sat-scores-fall-behind

Aronson, J., & Inzlicht, M. (2004). The ups and downs of attributional ambiguity: Stereotype vulnerability and the academic self-knowledge of African American college students. *Psychological Science, 15*(12), 829–836. http://www.jstor.org/stable/40064055

Baker, E. (2006). Meyerhoff scholarship program. In M. J. Cuyjet (Ed.), *African American men in college*. Jossey-Bass.

Bandura, A. (1986). *Social foundations of thought and action: A social cognitive theory*. Prentice-Hall, Inc.

Banks, C. A. (2009). *Black women undergraduates, cultural capital, and college success*. Peter Lang Publishing.

Bell, D. A. (1992). *Faces at the bottom of the well: The permanence of racism*. Basic Books.

Bledsoe, T., & Rome, K. D. (2006). Student African American brotherhood. In M. J. Cuyjet (Ed.), *African American men in college*. Jossey-Bass.

Bogdan, R., & Biklen, S. K. (Eds.). (1982). *Qualitative research for education: An introduction to theory and methods*. Allyn and Bacon.

Bonner, F. A., II. (2001). *Gifted African American male college students: A phenomenological study*. National Research Center for the Gifted and Talented.

Bonner, F. A., & Bailey, K. W. (2006). Enhancing the academic climate for African American men. In M. J. Cuyjet (Ed.), *African American men in college*. Jossey-Bass.

Borland, J. H. (2004). *Issues and practices in the identification and education of gifted students from under-represented groups* (RM04186). The National Research Center on the Gifted and Talented, University of Connecticut. Retrieved February 10, 2015, from http://www.gifted.uconn.edu/nrcgt/borland.html

Brown, S. (2019, February 14). Nearly half of undergraduates are students of color. But Black students lag behind. *The Chronicle of Higher Education*. https://www-chronicle-com.proxy.libraries.rutgers.edu/article/nearly-half-of-undergraduates-are-students-of-color-but-black-students-lag-behind/

Byrd, J. A., & Porter, C. J. (2022). Black undergraduate women navigating (mis)representation, strength, and strategies: An analysis of influences on their mental wellness. In L. D. Patton, V. E. Evans-Winters, & C. E. Jacobs (Eds.), *Investing in the educational success of Black women and girls* (pp. 175–191). Stylus.

Carter, P. L. (2006). Straddling boundaries: Identity, culture, and school. *Sociology of Education, 79*(4), 304–328. http://www.jstor.org/stable/25054322

Cho, S., Crenshaw, K. W., & McCall, L. (2013). Toward a field of intersectionality studies: Theory, applications, and praxis. *Signs, 38*(4) (Intersectionality: Theorizing Power, Empowering Theory), 785–810. http://www.jstor.org/stable/10.1086/669608

Choo, H. Y., & Ferree, M. M. (2010). Practicing intersectionality in sociological research: A critical analysis of inclusions, interactions, and institutions in the study of inequalities. *Sociological Theory, 28*(2), 129–149. https://doi.org/10.1111/j.1467-9558.2010.01370.x

Chwalisz, K., & Greer, T. M. (2007). Minority-related stressors and coping processes among African American college students. *Journal of College Student Development, 48*(4), 388–404. https://doi.org/10.1353/csd.2007.0037

Cole, E. R. (2009). Intersectionality and research in psychology. *American Psychologist, 64*(3), 170–80.

Coleman, L. L., & Kotinek, J. D. (Eds). (2010). *Setting the table for diversity*. National Collegiate Honors Council.

Collins, P. H. (1991/2000). *Black feminist thought: Knowledge, consciousness, and the politics of empowerment*. Routledge.

Collins, P. H. (1998). *Fighting words: Black women and the search for justice*. (No. 7). University of Minnesota Press.

Collins, P. H. (2012). Social inequality, power, and politics: Intersectionality and American pragmatism in dialogue. *The Journal of Speculative Philosophy, 26*(2), 442–457. https://doi.org/10.1007/BF01112192

Collins, P. H. (2015). Intersectionality's definitional dilemmas. *Annual Review of Sociology, 41*, 1–20. https://doi.org/10.1146/annurev-soc-073014-112142

Comeaux, E. (2013). Faculty perceptions of high-achieving male collegians: A critical race theory analysis. *Journal of College Student Development, 54*(5), 453–465.

Commodore, F., Baker, D., & Arroyo, A. (2018). *Black women college students: A guide to student success in higher education*. Routledge.

Crenshaw, K. W. (1989). Toward a race-conscious pedagogy in legal education. *National Black Law Journal, 11*(1), 1.

Crenshaw, K. (1991). Mapping the margins: Intersectionality, identity politics, and violence against women of color. *Stanford Law Review, 43*(6), 1241–1299. http://www.jstor.org/stable/1229039

Creswell, J. W. (2009). *Research design: Qualitative, quantitative, and mixed methods approaches* (3rd ed.). Sage Publications.

Cuyjet, M. J. (Ed.). (2006). *African American men in college*. Jossey-Bass.

Davis, A. M. (2018). Not so gifted: Academic identity for Black women in honors. *Journal of the National Collegiate Honors Council, 19.2.*

Denzin, N. K., & Giardina, M. D. (2007). *Ethical futures in qualitative research: Decolonizing the politics of knowledge.* Left Coast Press.

Donahoo. S. (2017). An examination of black women as students in college films: Where my girls at? In *Critical Perspectives on Black Women and College Success* (pp. 59–74). https://doi.org/10.4324/9781315744421

Donovan, R. A., & Guillory, N. A. (2017). Black women's college experience: Influence of sociostructural stressors. In L. D. Patton & N. N. Croom (Eds.), *Critical perspectives on Black women and college success* (pp. 188–199). Routledge.

Durkee, M., Gazley, E., Hope, E., & Keels, M. (2019). Cultural invalidations: Deconstructing the "acting white" phenomenon among Black and Latinx college students. *Cultural Diversity & Ethnic Minority Psychology, 25,* 451–460. https://doi.org/10.1037/cdp0000288

Evans, N. J., Forney, D. S., & Guido-DiBrito, F. (1998). *Student development in college: Theory, research, and practice.* Jossey-Bass Publishers.

Everett, K. D. & Croom, N. N. (2017). From discourse to practice: Making discourses about black undergraduate womyn visible in higher education journals and student affairs practice. In *Critical Perspectives on Black Women and College Success* (pp. 75–87). Routledge. https://doi.org/10.4324/9781315744421

Fordham, S., & Ogbu, J. (1986). Black students' school success: Coping with the burden of acting white. *The Urban Review, 18*(3), 176–206. https://doi.org/10.1007/BF01112192

Freeman, K. (1999). No services needed?: The case for mentoring high-achieving African American students. *Peabody Journal of Education, 74*(2), 15–26.

Fries-Britt, S. (1998). Moving beyond achiever isolation: Experiences of gifted Black collegians. *Journal of Higher Education, 69*(5), 556–576.

Fries-Britt, S. (2002). High-achieving Black collegians. *About Campus, 7*(3), 2–8.

Fries-Britt, S., & Griffin, K. A. (2007). The Black box: How high-achieving Blacks resist stereotypes about Black Americans. *Journal of College Student Development, 48*(5), 509–524. http://search.proquest.com.libproxy.temple.edu/docview/195181552?accountid=14270

Fries-Britt, S. L., & Turner, B. (2001). Facing stereotypes: A case study of Black students on a white campus. *Journal of College Student Development, 42*(5), 420. http://search.proquest.com.libproxy.temple.edu/docview/195178510?accountid=14270

Gaither, G. H. (2005). *Minority retention: What works?* Jossey-Bass.

Gold, S. P. (2011). Buried treasure: Community cultural wealth among Black American female students. Support systems and services for diverse populations: Considering the intersection of race, gender, and the needs of Black female undergraduates. *Diversity in Higher Education, 8*, 59–72.

Grier-Reed, T. (2013). The African American student network: An informal networking group as a therapeutic intervention for black college students on a predominantly white campus. *Journal of Black Psychology, 39*(2), 169–184. https://doi.org/10.1177/0095798413478696Griffin, K. (2006). Striving for success: A qualitative exploration of competing theories of high-achieving black college students' academic motivation. *Journal of College Student Development, 47*(4), 384–400. https://doi.org/10.1353/csd.2006.0045

Hancock, A. (2007). Intersectionality as a normative and empirical paradigm. *Politics & Gender, 3*(2), 248–254. https://doi.org/10.1017/S1743923X07000062

Harper, S. R. (2005). Leading the way: Inside the experiences of high-achieving African American male students. *About Campus, 10*(1), 8–15.

Harper, S. R., & Quaye, S. J. (2007). Student organizations as venues for Black identity expression and development among African American male student leaders. *Journal of College Student Development, 48*(2), 127–144. http://search.proquest.com /docview/195177904?accountid=14270

Harris-Perry, M. V. (2011). *Sister citizen: Shame, stereotypes, and Black women in America*. Yale University Press.

Hesse-Biber, S. N., & Leavy, P. (2011). *The practice of qualitative research*. Sage Publications.

Hoggard, L. S., Byrd, C. M., & Sellers, R. M. (2012). Comparison of African American college students' coping with racially and nonracially stressful events. *Cultural Diversity & Ethnic Minority Psychology, 18*(4), 329–339. https://doi.org/10.1037/a0029437

Hooks, b. (2014). *Teaching to transgress education as the practice of freedom*. Taylor and Francis. https://doi.org/10.4324 /9780203700280

Inzlicht, M., & Ben-Zeev, T. (2003). Do high-achieving female students underperform in private? The implications of threatening environments on intellectual processing. *Journal of Educational Psychology, 95*(4), 796.

Jaschik (2015, September 3). SAT scores drop. *InsideHigherEd.com*. https://www.insidehighered.com/news/2015/09/03/sat-scores -drop-and-racial-gaps-remain-large

Jerald, M. C., Cole, E. R., Ward, L. M., & Avery, L. R. (2017, October). Controlling images: How awareness of group stereotypes affects black women's well-being. *Journal of Counseling Psychology, 64*(5), 487–499.

Johnson, J. M. (2017). Choosing elites: Experiences of working-class Black undergraduate women at an Ivy League university. In L. D. Patton & N. N. Croom (Eds.), *Critical perspectives on Black women and college success* (pp. 188–199). Routledge.

Jordan-Zachery, J. S. (2007). Am I a black woman or a woman who is black? A few thoughts on the meaning of intersectionality. *Politics & Gender, 3*(02), 254–263. https://doi.org/10.1017/S1743923X07000074

Joseph, N. M. (2022). Institutionalized efforts to increase the participation of black women and girls in STEM. In L. D. Patton, V. E. Evans-Winters, & C. E. Jacobs (Eds.), *Investing in the educational success of Black women and girls* (pp. 40–58). Stylus.

Kane, L., & Kiersz, A. (2015, April 9). Here's what you have to earn to be considered middle class in the 50 biggest US cities, *Business Insider.* https://www.businessinsider.com.au/what-middle-class-means-in-50-major-us-cities-2015-4

Kanter, J. W., Williams, M. T., Kuczynski, A. M., Manbeck, K. E., Debreaux, M., & Rosen, D. C. (2017). A preliminary report on the relationship between microaggressions against Black people and racism among white college students. *Race and Social Problems, 9*, 291–299. https://doi-org.proxy.libraries.rutgers.edu/10.1007/s12552-017-9214-0

Lewis, J. A., Mendenhall, R., Harwood, S. A., & Huntt, M. B. (2012). Coping with gendered racial microaggressions among Black women college students. *Journal of African American Studies, 17*, 51–73. https://doi.org/10.1007/s12111-012-9219-0

Lichtman, M. (2010). *Qualitative research in education: A user's guide.* Sage Publications.

Massey, D. S., Mooney, M., Torres, K. C., & Charles, C. Z. (2007). Black immigrants and Black natives attending selective colleges and universities in the United States. *American Journal of Education, 113*(2), 243–271.

Miles, M. B., & Huberman, A. M. (1994). *Qualitative data analysis: An expanded sourcebook.* Sage Publications.

More Blacks are competing in Advanced Placement programs, but the racial scoring gap is widening. (2008). *Journal of Blacks in Higher Education.* http://www.jbhe.com/features/59_apscoringgap.html

Mwangi, C.A.G., & Fries-Britt, S. (2015). Black within black: The perceptions of black immigrant collegians and their U.S. college experience. *About Campus*, *20*(2), 16–23. https://doi.org/10.1002/abc.21187

Nasir, N. S., McLaughlin, M. W., & Jones, A. (2009). What does it mean to be African American? Constructions of race and academic identity in an urban public high school. *American Educational Research Journal*, *46*(1), 73–114. https://doi.org/10.3102/0002831208323279

National Center for Education Statistics. (2020). Characteristics of Postsecondary Faculty. In *The Condition of Education*. https://nces.ed.gov/programs/coe/pdf/coe_csc.pdf

Njoku, N. R., & Patton, L. D. (2017). Explorations of respectability and resistance in constructions of Black womanhood at HBCUs. In L. D. Patton & N. N. Croom (Eds.), *Critical perspectives on Black women and college success* (pp. 143–157). Routledge.

Núñez, A. (2014). Employing multilevel intersectionality in educational research: Latino identities, contexts, and college access. *Educational Researcher*, *43*(2), 85–92. https://doi.org/10.3102/0013189X14522320

Ogbu, J. U. (2004). Collective identity and the burden of 'acting white' in black history, community, and education. *The Urban Review, 36*, 1–35.

Palmer, R. T., Wood, J. L., & Arroyo, A. (2015). Toward a model of retention and persistence for Black men at historically Black colleges and universities (HBCUs). *Spectrum* (Bloomington, Ind.: 2012), *4*(1), 5–20. https://doi.org/10.2979/spectrum.4.1.02

Pascarella, E. T. (1980). Student-faculty informal contact and college outcomes. *Review of Educational Research, 50*(4), 545–595.

Pascarella, E. T., & Terenzini, P. T. (2005). *How college affects students: A third decade of research*. Jossey-Bass.

Patton, L. D. (2022). Introduction: Establishing a context for studying Black women and girls in education. In L. D. Patton, V. E. Evans-Winters, & C. E. Jacobs (Eds.), *Investing in the educational success of Black women and girls* (pp. 1–8). Stylus.

Patton, L. D., Copridge, K., & Sharp, S. (2022). Black women undergraduates' reflections on the pathway to college: Naming and challenging structural disinvestments. In L. D. Patton, V. E. Evans-Winters, C. E. Jacobs (Eds.), *Investing in the educational success of Black women and girls* (pp. 145–159). Stylus.

Patton, L. D., & Croom, N. N. (2017). *Critical perspectives on Black women and college success.* Routledge.

Patton, L. D., Evans-Winters, V. E., & Jacobs, C. E. (2022). *Investing in the educational success of Black women and girls.* Stylus.

Pearson, B., & Kohl, D. (2010). African American males and honors programs: Why are enrollments so low? What can be done? In *Setting the table for diversity* (pp. 31–30). National Collegiate Honors Council.

Porter, C. J. (2017). Articulation of identity in Black undergraduate women: Influences, interactions, and intersections. In L. D. Patton & N. N. Croom (Eds.), *Critical perspectives on Black women and college success* (pp. 88–100). Routledge.

Porter, C. J., & Dean, L. A. (2015). Making meaning: Identity development of black undergraduate women. *NASPA Journal about Women in Higher Education, 8*(2), 125–139. https://doi.org/10.1080/19407882.2015.1057164

Porter, C. J., Green, Q., Daniels, M., & Smota, M. (2020). Black women's socialization and identity development in college: Advancing Black Feminist Thought. *Journal of College Student Affairs Research and Practice, 57*(3), 253–265. https://doi.org/10.1080/19496591.2019.1683021

Robinson, T., & Williams, B. (2022). Still retaining each other: Black women building community through social media and other digital platforms. In L. D. Patton, V. E. Evans-Winters, & C. E. Jacobs (Eds.), *Investing in the educational success of Black women and girls* (pp. 258–275). Stylus.

Sanders, M. G. (1997). Overcoming obstacles: Academic achievement as a response to racism and discrimination. *The Journal of Negro Education, 66*(1), 83.

Sanon-Jules, L. B. (2010). How honors programs can assist in the transition of gifted first-generation and African American college students. In *Setting the table for diversity* (pp. 99–114). National Collegiate Honors Council.

Sax, L. J., Byrant, A. N., & Harper, C. E. (2005). The differential effects of student-faculty interaction on college outcomes for women and men. *Journal of College Student Development, 46*(6), 642–657. https://doi.org/10.1353/csd.2005.0067

Seidman, I. (2006). *Interviewing as qualitative research: A guide for researchers in education and the social sciences.* Teachers College Press.

Sellers, R., Chavous, T., & Cooke, D. (1998). Racial ideology and racial centrality as predictors of African American college students' academic performance. *Journal of Black Psychology, 1*(24): 8–27. http://hdl.handle.net/2027.42/68124

Sellers, R., & Shelton, J. (2003). The role of racial identity in perceived racial discrimination. *Journal of Personality and Social Psychology, 84*(5), 1079–1092. https://doi.org/10.1037/0022-3514.84.5.1079

Shaw, M. D. (2017). Supporting students who struggle successfully: Developing and institutionalizing support for Black undergraduate women. In L. D. Patton & N. N. Croom (Eds.), *Critical perspectives on Black women and college success* (pp. 188–199). Routledge.

Solórzano, D., Ceja, M., & Yosso, T. (2000). Critical race theory, racial microaggressions, and campus racial climate: The experiences of African American college students. *The Journal of Negro Education, 69*(1/2), 60–73.

Spencer, M. B., Noll, E., Stoltzfus, J., & Harpalani, V. (2001). Identity and school adjustment: Questioning the "Acting White" assumption. *Educational Psychologist, 36*(1), 21–30.

Steele, C. (2010). *Whistling Vivaldi: And other clues to how stereotypes affect us.* W. W. Norton & Company.

Steele, C. M., & Aronson, J. (1995). Stereotype threat and the intellectual test performance of African Americans. *Journal of Personality and Social Psychology*, 69, 797–811.

Steele, T. J. (2022). "Staying out the way": Connecting Black girls' experiences with school discipline to collegiate experiences. In L. D. Patton, V. E. Evans-Winters, & C. E. Jacobs (Eds.), *Investing in the educational success of Black women and girls* (pp. 1–8). Stylus.

Stewart, D. L. (2009). Perceptions of multiple identities among black college students. *Journal of College Student Development*, 50(3), 253–270.

Stewart, D. L. (2017). (In)visibility, involvement, and success: A counternarrative of Black women in predominantly white liberal arts colleges, 1945–1965. In L. D. Patton & N. N. Croom (Eds.), *Critical perspectives on Black women and college success* (pp. 31–43). Routledge.

Strayhorn, T. L. (2009). The burden of proof: A quantitative study of high-achieving Black collegians. *Journal of African American Studies*, 13(4), 375–387. https://doi.org/10.1007/s12111-008-9059-0

Strayhorn, T. L., & DeVita, J. M. (2010). African American males' student engagement: A comparison of good practices by institutional type. *Journal of African American Studies*, 14, 87–105. https://doi.org/10.1007/s12111-009-9110-9

Strayhorn, T. L., & Johnson, R. M. (2014). Why are all the white students sitting together in college? Impact of Brown v. Board of Education on cross-racial interactions among Blacks and Whites. *The Journal of Negro Education*, 83(3), 385–399. https://doi.org/10.7709/jnegroeducation.83.3.0385

Swim, J. K., Hyers, L. L., Cohen, L. L., Fitzgerald, D. C., & Bylsma, W. H. (2003). African American college students' experiences with everyday racism: Characteristics of and responses to these incidents. *Journal of Black Psychology*, 29(1), 38–67. https://doi.org/10.1177/0095798402239228

Teddlie, C., & Tashakkori, A. (Eds.). (2009). *Foundations of mixed methods research: Integrating quantitative and qualitative approaches in the social and behavioral sciences*. Sage Publications.

Tinto, V. (1975). Dropout from higher education: A theoretical synthesis of recent research. *Review of Educational Research, 45*(1), 89–125. http://www.jstor.org/stable/1170024

Tinto, V. (2000). Taking retention seriously: Rethinking the first year of college. *NACADA Journal, 19*(2), 5–10.

Umbach, P. D., & Wawryznski, M. R. (2005). Faculty do matter: the role of college faculty in student learning and engagement. *Research in Higher Education, 46*(2), 153–184. https://doi.org/10.1007/s11162-004-1598-1

Walley-Jean, J. C. (2009). Debunking the myth of the "angry Black woman": An exploration of anger in young African American women. *Black Women, Gender Families, 3*(2), 68–86. http://www.jstor.org/stable/10.5406/blacwomegendfami.3.2.0068

West, L. M., Donovan, R. A., & Daniel, A. R. (2016). The price of strength: Black college women's perspectives on the strong Black woman stereotype. *Women & Therapy, 39*, 390–412.

West, L. M., Donovan, R. A., & Roemer, L. (2009). Coping with racism: What works and doesn't work for black women? *The Journal of Black Psychology, 36*(3), 331–349. http://dx.doi.org/10.1177/0095798409353755

Williams, P. J. (1998). *Seeing a color-blind future: The paradox of race*. Noonday Press.

Williamson, M. (1996). *A return to love: Reflections on the principles of a course in miracles*. HarperCollins.

Winkle-Wagner, R. (2009). *The unchosen me: Race, gender, and identity among black women in college*. The Johns Hopkins University Press.

Winkle-Wagner, R., Kelly, B., Luedke, C., & Reavis, T. (2019). Authentically me: Examining expectations that are placed upon Black women in college. *American Educational Research Journal, 56*(2), 407–443. https://doi.org/10.3102/0002831218798326

Wood, J. L., & Palmer, R. T. (2015). *Black men in higher education: A guide to ensuring student success*. Routledge.

Yip, T., Seaton, E. K., & Sellers, R. M. (2006). African American racial identity across the lifespan: Identity status, identity content, and depressive symptoms. *Child Development, 77*(5), 1504–1517. https://doi.org/10.1111/j.1467-8624.2006.00950.x

Zamani, E. M. (2003). African American women in higher education. *New Directions for Student Services*, 2003(104), 5–18. https://doi.org/10.1002/ss.103

Zamani-Gallaher, E. M. & Polite, V. C. (2013). *African American females: Addressing challenges and nurturing the future*. Michigan State University Press.

Zamudio, M. M., & Rios, F. (2006). From traditional to liberal racism: Living racism in the everyday. *Sociological Perspectives, 49*(4), 483–501. https://doi.org/10.1525/sop.2006.49.4.483

Index

About the Author

ADRIANNE MUSU DAVIS, PHD, is administrative dean/director of the honors program in the School of Arts and Sciences at Rutgers University. She is also an education consultant and speaker. She has been a higher education practitioner-scholar for over fifteen years. Her research interests focus on experiences and identities of Black women and other minoritized students and high-achievers; and race and inclusion in academic contexts, particularly in higher education. She lives outside Philadelphia with her family.

Yang Va Lor, *Unequal Choices: How Social Class Shapes Where High-Achieving Students Apply to College*

Dana M. Malone, *From Single to Serious: Relationships, Gender, and Sexuality on American Evangelical Campuses*

Z. Nicolazzo, Alden Jones, and Sy Simms, *Digital Me: Trans Students Exploring Future Possible Selves Online*

Nathanael J. Okpych, *Climbing a Broken Ladder: Contributors of College Success for Youth in Foster Care*

A. Fiona Pearson, *Back in School: How Student Parents Are Transforming College and Family*

Barrett J. Taylor and Brendan Cantwell, *Unequal Higher Education: Wealth, Status, and Student Opportunity*

James M. Thomas, *Diversity Regimes: Why Talk Is Not Enough to Fix Racial Inequality at Universities*

Printed in the United States
by Baker & Taylor Publisher Services